From the Tip of My Tongue

From the Tip of My Tongue

Stories and Recipes
From One of Florida's Favorite Chefs

By Cindy Hutson with Jen Karetnick

Photographs by Michael Pisarri
Design by Albert Chiang

story farm

Winter Park · Miami · Santa Barbara · Honolulu

From the Tip of My Tongue
© 2015 by Cindy Hutson

Photographs © 2015 by Michael Pisarri

Published in the United States by Story Farm, LLC.
www.story-farm.com

Library of Congress Cataloging-in-Publication Data
is available upon request.

ISBN: 978-0-9905205-4-2

PRINTED IN CHINA

EDITORIAL DIRECTOR: Ashley Fraxedas
ART DIRECTOR: Albert Chiang
PROJECT MANAGER: Ashley Hutson
PHOTO STYLING: Joy Moore
COPY EDITOR: Eva Dougherty
INDEXING: Amy Hall
PRODUCTION MANAGEMENT: Tina Dahl

10 9 8 7 6 5 4 3 2 1

FIRST EDITION

For my love—Delius Shirley.
I thank you for walking me down a path I would not have taken
had I never met you. There is something very special
about finding your true calling in life. Thank you for giving me
the confidence in myself to follow through.

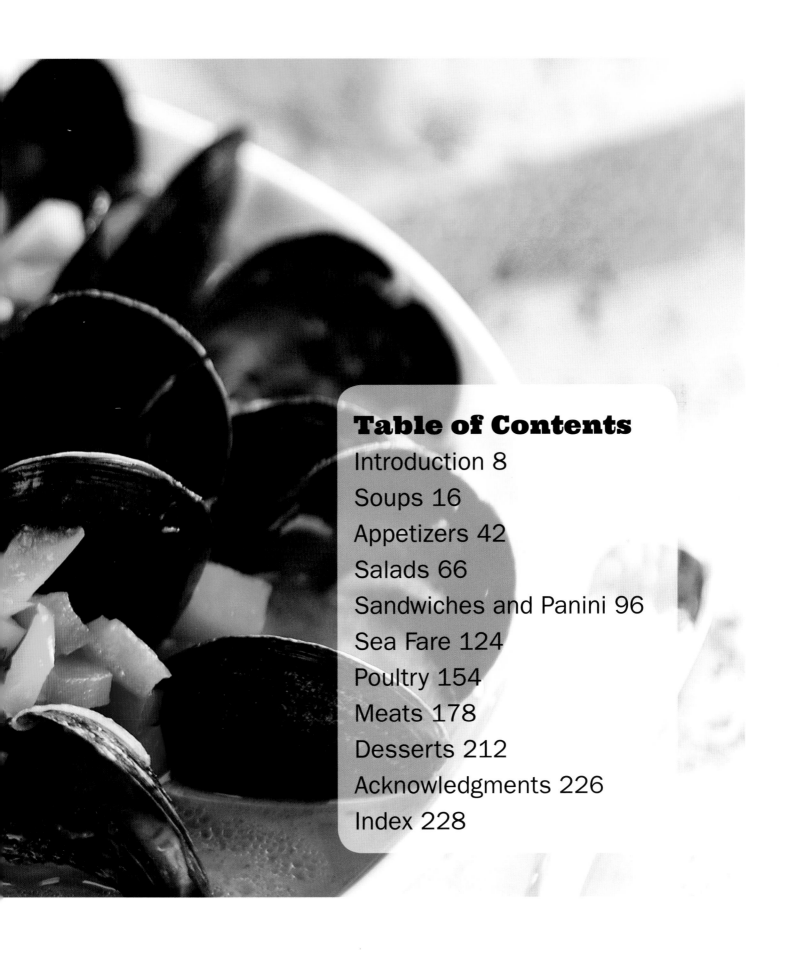

Table of Contents

The Tip of My Tongue

From the time I could crawl, eating was my curiosity, my comfort and my mischief. I would eat anything. My parents had to pump my stomach more times than they had to pump those of our dogs, who had a passion for eating everyone's socks. They always told stories of how I would sprinkle out the insides of the TAT brand of ant traps; apparently it was a poison that to me tasted like cake. Or about how they would find me crawling on the back patio with half of a woolly bear caterpillar hanging out of my mouth. Those tiny, wiggly, green inchworms that descended on silken threads in summer, high from the trees, became my snacks as well, once they reached my fisted little mitt. And while I wasn't old enough to speak my disapproval when my mother swiped the remains of whatever tasty treat I had found from my mouth with her forefinger, I could certainly scream bloody murder.

As it was evident from that very young age that I had an adventurous palate—unlike my sister, Kathy, and brothers John and Eddie—I was never forced to order from children's menus at restaurants. Nor did I want to. Instead, I was right next to my father eating clams on the half shell, smoked oysters on saltines, liver and onions

on rye bread with mustard, garlic-sautéed frog's legs and whole Jersey tomatoes, bitten into like an apple, with salt and pepper and juice dripping down my arms and face. My father would also allow me to have green crème de menthe and vanilla ice-cream parfaits, which would make my mom hit the ceiling. "Jack!" she would scream. "You can't give a 5-year-old alcohol!"

My mother, well, she really hated to cook. If she were stuck in the kitchen cooking, she couldn't be out front, hanging with all of us kids and our friends, having fun. And our house was the "fun house." All the neighborhood children always wanted to come over to our house, and Mom and Dad always said things like "The more, the merrier" and "Sure, they can eat over."

Sometimes, though, our friends got smart and asked, "Who's cooking, your mom or your dad?" See, they knew that if Dad was on duty, that night's meal might be great steaks on the grill or barbecued chicken and corn on the cob. But if it were Mom, she'd want to speed things up and get out of the kitchen, so it'd be Green Giant Niblets corn in boil bags snipped open, Stove Top stuffing and dry chicken. If we complained about having chicken all the time, she'd say, "I don't see any of you getting skinny over it." Then, one day, my brother John's friends Gary, Teddy and Kenny bought our mom a book as a joke: *101 Ways to Cook Chicken.* She was a great sport, and always took her culinary ridicule with a grain of salt.

On the other hand, if we told her we liked something, it meant we'd never have it again. She would just strike it from her recipe list. My sister Kathy and I could never figure that out. In retrospect, our best guess is that she wanted Dad to cook more often, and if she made food we all hated, he would.

Back then, however, we couldn't figure out why Mom wasn't a good cook, because her mother and father sure could make some great food. We called them Ma and Pa, and it was with Pa that I shared some of my most memorable vacations in the Florida Panhandle as a little girl. He and I were always the first up, and out we would go in the dark on his skiff, *Easy Bee*, in order to meet the shrimpers, who'd sell us buckets of shrimp for just five measly dollars each.

After that, we checked the crab traps at the end of the dock that we'd filled with gray mullet and chicken necks the night before. They were always loaded with pissed-off crabs. We had to carefully dodge their vicious pincers as they waved like angry aliens, trying to take our fingers off. Pa taught me how to grab

them by the two back flipper fins to keep from being snagged by their pit bull-like death grips. We also had to find the females with their underside aprons bulging with their spongy eggs, and set them free. He only allowed us to keep the big males.

Pa taught me how to clean the crabs standing in the bay, calf-deep in water. As all the lungs and guts came out of the crabs, schools of little fish would come in to nibble our feet, and sometimes some more live crabs would show up and have me scurrying out of the water, screaming. At that point, the sun would be coming up on Santa Rosa Sound. It was always so beautiful to me, but Pa never failed to say, "Red sky at night, sailors delight. Red sky in the morning, sailors take warning."

Some days, when the tide was right, we would go to the sandbar with our old sneakers on and a big tin bucket fixed in a tire tube, carrying hand nets. This is how we went scalloping. He taught me to gently bury the tips of my sneakers in the sand and watch closely for the bay scallops to emerge, pulsing themselves backward. We then reached behind them with the nets and let them propel themselves into their own captivity. They were delicious and so pretty, with a band of what looked like eyes around the entire edges of their shells, which themselves were a stunning, iridescent turquoise, pink, green and mother-of-pearl.

These wonderful treasures from Santa Rosa Bay became our amazing breakfast that Pa and I cooked just before the household awoke. He basted sunny-side-up eggs perfectly in the bacon grease that he pooled in his tilted electric frying pan. I stood on a stepstool and was in charge of dipping those sweet-smelling scallops in egg wash and his cornmeal dust. They took an instant to cook. We also dipped the fresh shrimp in the cornmeal.

If the fig tree had fresh fruit on it, figs went on the table too, along with grits. This was a Southern breakfast feast, and it was a place very special to me always, a place of gatherings and family and food.

As I grew, so did my love for cooking. I had become very chubby as a child, and really began to despise eating processed foods. After all, I lived in New Jersey, the Garden State. We were close to farms and orchards, pastures and gardens. It was the country, and I wanted to eat things from there. I began watching *The Galloping Gourmet* and Chef Tell on television after school. I loved them, thinking, "Look how much fun they are having cooking," and drawing parallels with the fact that I had fun cooking too. So I would watch the shows and have Mom go to the A&P in Berkeley Heights and buy some ingredients and cook what I saw Graham Kerr make. I also cooked recipes off the backs of Baker's chocolate or Bisquick boxes. Sometimes friends would be outside playing kickball and I would be inside making fudge. When I was done and the fudge was setting, only then would I head outside.

Still, while I would emulate those chefs, it never occurred to me to become a chef. I just loved cooking and seeing the satisfaction on the faces of people who ate my food. In my early teens, I met a girl named June D'Ascoli, who would rapidly become my closest friend. I spent a lot of time at her house. Her father, "Checky," was a chef and restaurateur, and her mother, Vilma, and her grandmother, who spoke no English, were also always doing something revolving around food. That house smelled amazing at all times. I watched Checky and his food very closely. He ate one meal at home per day, and it consisted of so many fresh, wonderfully prepared Italian dishes, that I never knew where to begin when I was invited to eat there. I was a little bit afraid too, because it seemed like everyone was always yelling, and they were. But when I would ask June why they were fighting, she would say, "They're not fighting!" Eventually, my hunger overtook my fear and I dove into freshly steamed artichoke hearts and garlic or bacalao. It was here I began cooking Italian food, and I still love cooking it to this day.

I left New Jersey in 1978 in search of sunny skies and adventure. Having learned to fish from my dad and Pa and my brother Eddie, I let my fingers do the walking through the yellow pages and found a place to get my "six-pack captain's license," which meant I could charter my own boat, taking out six or fewer people in a boat no bigger than 65 feet. I married shortly after that to my first husband, Richard, and we had a child together, Justin. We spent several years that way, sport fishing on 28-, 31- and then 33-foot Bertrams, me in a bikini, kite fishing and trolling most days for wahoo, mahi-mahi, billfish and more.

Female boat captains were a rarity in those days, and when we'd bring in 50 to 100 mahi-mahi and I got to work filleting them on the dock, I'd always draw a crowd. It was like I was an attraction. Simply put, I had a blast. What I also had was the freshest fish, which I sold to local fish markets. I also kept some to cook or eat raw with family and friends. Everyone wanted me to cook at their parties, and in those days we had plenty of them. Life wasn't always a party—my marriage to Richard dissolved when our son was 3. But by then I had met Iris Day, also known as the Jamaican Dragon Lady, and her daughter Rosalie. I never suspected the important role that those two ladies would play in my life.

Iris, Rosalie and I spent many years cooking, creating dishes and socializing the island way. I just loved it, but it was more than that. Everything about Jamaican island life felt like second nature to me—the people, the history, the cuisine. I was intrigued and fascinated by it all. Rosalie was the one who introduced me to Charles Hutson, who eventually became my second husband. His family and the Jamaican lifestyle we led were wonderful. I thoroughly enjoyed entertaining and cooking for them. Jamaicans are great for just showing up at any given time, which is when, of course, the cooking begins. It was very similar to the life I had led growing up with my parents—for me, the more, the merrier—but this ver-

sion included curried chicken, rice and peas, callaloo and Jimmy Hutson's famous rum punch—a rum punch that was dubbed, for probably obvious reason, "the fighting rum punch."

Charles and I had two beautiful "Jamerican" children, Christian and Ashley. But that marriage too had started to fail. That's about the time that I met Delius Shirley, son of the great chef Norma Shirley and anesthesiologist Michael Shirley. After helping his mother with her restaurant, managing her food costs and such, Delius was ready to leave the island. As a soon-to-be single mother of three children with no college education, but with a good deal of common sense, street smarts and people skills, I would need a job. Charles and I were going to close our Jamaican coffee and condiment importation/distribution company and divorce. Delius proposed that we open a restaurant together in South Beach, a part of Miami that was just beginning to see some renovation and revitalization.

For a while, we tried to get loans to lease a promising spot on what was then a crumbling Lincoln Road. We played all the angles—ethnicity, single woman, everything. But no one would touch us. Finally, Delius spoke to his father, who lent us the money to get the restaurant, which we named Norma's on the Beach. Dr. Shirley had full faith in his son's business savvy and he knew he could make this work.

Frankly, I wasn't as convinced. We built the location ourselves with the help of our dear friend Joe

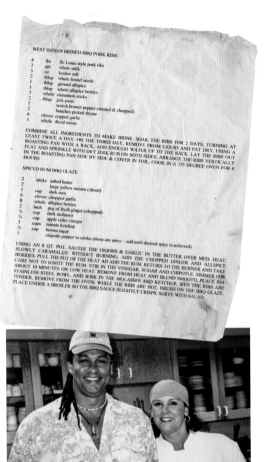

WEST INDIAN BRINED BBQ PORK RIBS

4	lbs	St. Louis style pork ribs
2	qts	whole milk
5	oz	kosher salt
2	tblsp	whole fennel seeds
1	tblsp	ground allspice
3	tblsp	whole allspice berries
3	whole	cinnamon sticks
2	tblsp	jerk paste
6		scotch bonnet pepper (seeded & chopped)
2		bunches picked thyme
6	cloves	copped garlic
1	whole	diced onion

COMBINE ALL INGREDIENTS TO MAKE BRINE. SOAK THE RIBS FOR 2 DAYS, TURNING AT LEAST TWICE A DAY. ON THE THIRD DAY, REMOVE FROM LIQUID AND PAT DRY. USING A ROASTING PAN WITH A RACK, ADD ENOUGH WATER UP TO THE RACK. LAY THE RIBS OUT FLAT AND SPRINKLE WITH DRY JERK RUB ON BOTH SIDES. ARRANGE THE RIBS VERTICALLY IN THE ROASTING PAN SIDE BY SIDE & COVER IN FOIL. COOK IN A 375 DEGREE OVEN FOR 4 HOURS

SPICED RUM BBQ GLAZE

2	sticks	salted butter
2		large yellow onions (sliced)
6	cup	dark rum
8	cloves	chopped garlic
2	whole	allspice berries
¾	inch	peg of fresh ginger (chopped)
¼	cup	dark molasses
3	cup	apple cider vinegar
½	cups	tomato ketchup
1	cup	brown sugar
		chipotle pepper in adobo (these are spicy – add until desired spice is achieved)

USING AN 8 QT. POT, SAUTEE THE ONIONS & GARLIC IN THE BUTTER OVER MED. HEAT. SLOWLY CARAMALIZE WITHOUT BURNING. ADD THE CHOPPED GINGER AND ALLSPICE BERRIES. PULL THE POT OF THE HEAT AD ADD THE RUM. RETURN TO THE BURNER AND TAKE CARE NOT TO IGNITE THE RUM. STIR IN THE VINEGAR, SUGAR AND CHIPOTLE. SIMMER FOR ABOUT 10 MINUTES ON LOW HEAT. REMOVE FROM HEAT AND BLEND SMOOTH. PLACE INA STAINLESS STEEL BOWL, AND WISK IN THE MOLASSES AND KETCHUP. WEN THE RIBS ARE TENDER, REMOVE FROM THE OVEN. WHILE THE RIBS ARE HOT, BRUSH ON THE BBQ GLAZE. PLACE UNDER A BROILER SO THE BBQ SAUCE SLIGHTLY CRISPS. SERVE WITH SALAD.

Sindoni. As we got closer to our opening time, Delius looked at me and said, "Hey, have you thought about your menu?" I said, "What? The menu? Are you crazy, do you want to lose all of your father's money? I can cook, but not every night for hundreds of people. I wouldn't know how to orchestrate that or order for that." He said, "You'll learn, I can teach you."

And that's what he did, but it was so hard, I cried all the time. Fifteen hours a day, every day. I never thought I would last. Then the first review came out in *USA Today.* They said the restaurant was amazing. The writer called it "a jewel of the Caribbean on Lincoln Road." Delius simply said, "I told you that you could do this. Now stop crying."

We spent November 1994 through August 1999 in that spot on Lincoln Road. In 1996, we met Robert Johnson, who gave us the opportunity to expand our business into Coral Gables. Delius and I were offered our current spot on Miracle Mile by the city manager of Coral Gables. She and other local politicians wanted to bring businesses into the Gables that would revitalize this great neighborhood, and they liked the vibe we had contributed to Lincoln Road. Robert Johnson lent us the money to allow us to make that move from South Beach to Coral Gables.

The move turned out to be perfect for us. Coral Gables, also known as the City Beautiful, was the community we had been looking for. We opened Ortanique on the Mile in June 1999. Mr. Johnson also partnered with us in Ortanique Las Vegas and Ortanique D.C. We have since closed Vegas and D.C. but have just passed our 15th anniversary in Coral Gables, and also operate two additional restaurants in the Caribbean—one in the Bahamas, and one in the Cayman Islands.

Writing this book, though, I have to admit I've been second-guessing myself. Well, maybe not to the average eye. But I have been plagued by doubts, and I have hemmed and hawed with my ego, going back and forth about writing a more chef-driven cookbook. I think about what will be said by a chef who buys this: "Wow, look at all these shortcuts she takes!"

But then I recall all the phone calls I get, sometimes on a daily basis, sometimes during the middle of a busy dinner service, from home cooks asking me how I make my chili, or what goes in my jerk marinade, or "Cindy, quick, help, I need a sauce for fish, I'm entertaining in an hour!" The first title I actually came up with was "Telephone Recipes," and I conceived it as help for the home cook. Then I started thinking that I really am simply a glorified home cook. I am just a bit more fortunate to have had exposure to travel, to have been taught by other chefs, and to have been able to learn from their kitchens. And of course, I would not have even thought about being a professional chef if it weren't for Delius saying that I could be, for Michael Shirley financing our venture in the first place, and for Norma Shirley lending us her famous name.

So this book, *From the Tip of My Tongue,* pays homage to those home cooks who work all day doing something they may not be lucky enough to love, then come home and pull together luscious meals for family or friends. They take an extra step to buy our books and cook our creations. My hope is, by lending them these recipes and stories, they follow along for a while, and then, like I've done so many times with the help of so many others, they add a little this or take out some of that, create new flavors, and make the dishes their own.

SOUPS

CHAPTER 1

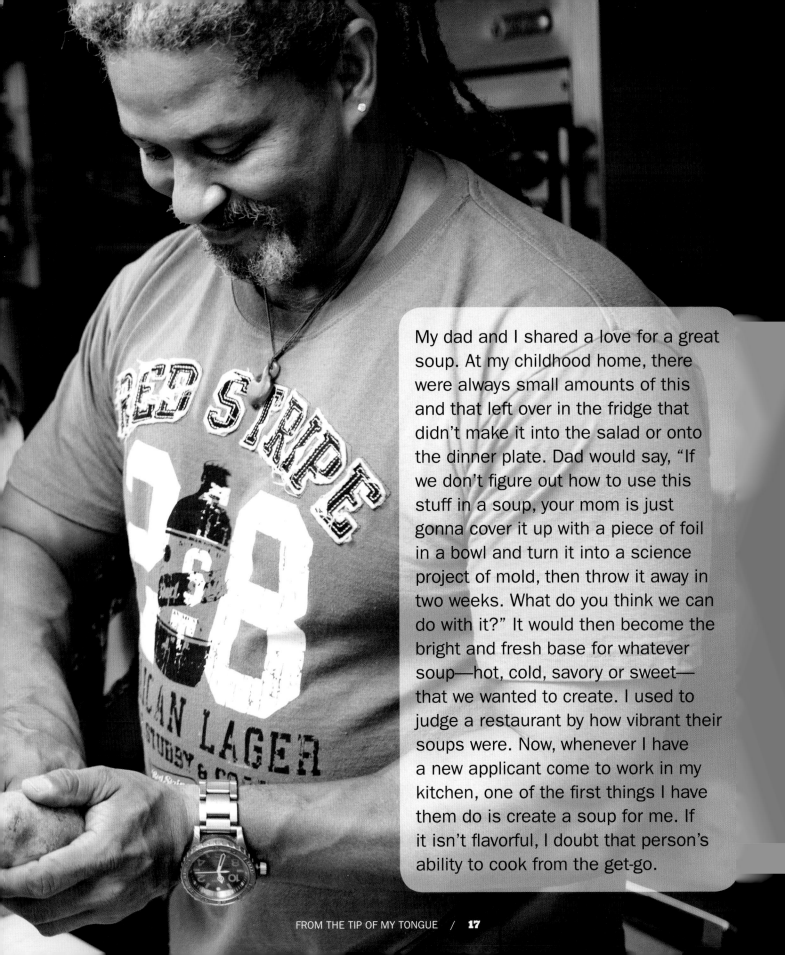

My dad and I shared a love for a great soup. At my childhood home, there were always small amounts of this and that left over in the fridge that didn't make it into the salad or onto the dinner plate. Dad would say, "If we don't figure out how to use this stuff in a soup, your mom is just gonna cover it up with a piece of foil in a bowl and turn it into a science project of mold, then throw it away in two weeks. What do you think we can do with it?" It would then become the bright and fresh base for whatever soup—hot, cold, savory or sweet—that we wanted to create. I used to judge a restaurant by how vibrant their soups were. Now, whenever I have a new applicant come to work in my kitchen, one of the first things I have them do is create a soup for me. If it isn't flavorful, I doubt that person's ability to cook from the get-go.

Bahamian-Style Conch Chowder

If you have ever had the good fortune of tasting fresh Bahamian conch straight out of the water, then you know what I am talking about when I say it is so sweet! I am lucky enough to be managing a restaurant in Harbour Island, Bahamas, at The Dunmore hotel. I've developed a good number of conch recipes there, and this is one of them. Although I can only bring freshly frozen conch back to the U.S. to serve at Ortanique, it still beats any conch I can find anywhere else in the world. I usually make extra of this soup because it is just one of those recipes you want seconds of.

SERVES TWELVE

2 rounded tablespoons Herb Butter (page 27)
1 cup brunoised yellow onion
2 cloves garlic, chopped
1 cup brunoised celery
1 cup diced carrots
3 cups diced potato
1 chayote squash, diced
1 Scotch bonnet chili pepper
2 tablespoons fresh thyme leaves
4 quarts clam juice
1 (14.5-ounce) can fire-roasted crushed tomatoes
3 cups diced vine-ripe tomatoes
3 pounds ground conch meat (see below)
2–3 tablespoons kosher salt

3 scallions, chopped
½ cup minced cilantro
Lime wedges

In a stockpot, melt butter. Sauté onion, garlic and celery until tender. Add carrots, potatoes, chayote, chili pepper and thyme and sauté until al dente.

Stir in the clam juice and bring to a boil. Add crushed tomatoes, vine-ripe tomatoes and ground conch, then reduce to a simmer, uncovered, for 15 minutes.

Remove chili pepper, slice open and scrape out seeds. Mince and return desired amount to soup according to spice tolerance. Salt soup to taste.

Pour into bowls and garnish each with scallion slices, cilantro and a squeeze of lime.

How to Grind Conch

In a food processor, grind the conch using the pulse button until there are no big pieces. Be careful not to overgrind because you will turn the conch into a pasty consistency.

Can't find conch? Use clams, shrimp, crab or a combo of all three. Serve it with a squeeze of lime, as above, and grilled bread with more Herb Butter.

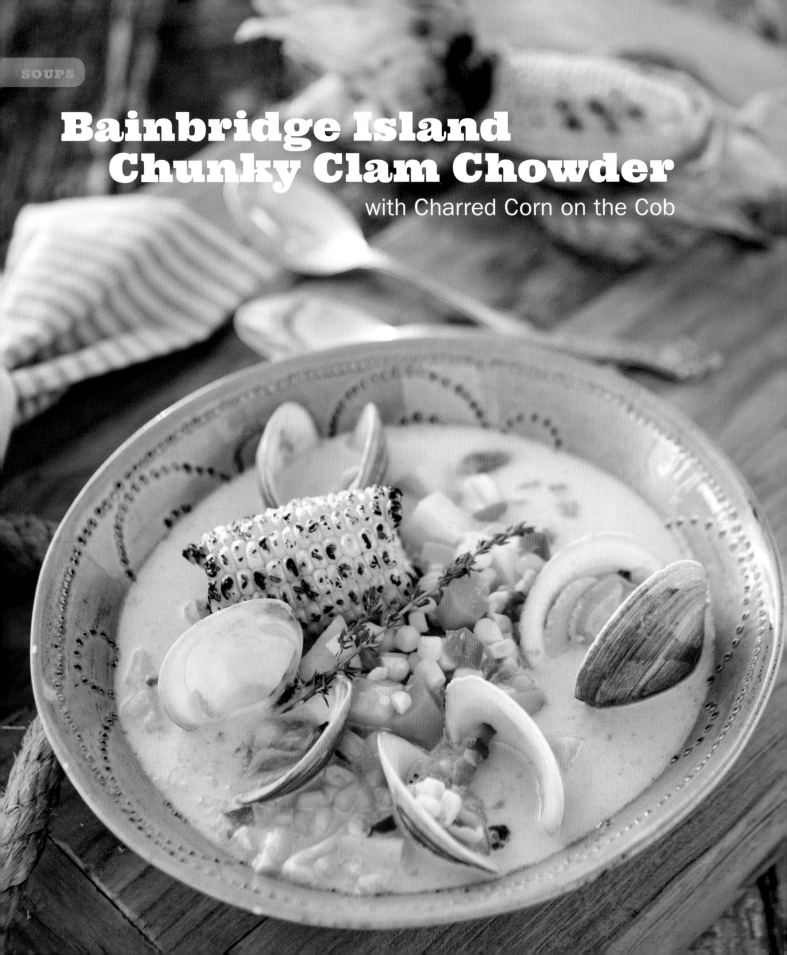

Bainbridge Island Chunky Clam Chowder

with Charred Corn on the Cob

My partner, Delius, and I went to Seattle one summer and decided to take some short trips to the surrounding islands resting in Puget Sound. Each one is amazing, offering its own personality. On Bainbridge Island, we came across this cool pub-style restaurant called Harbour Public House, where I had one of the best huge bowls of clam chowder that I've ever had. Paired with awesome bread, it was a meal in itself. I went back home to Miami thinking about that soup and decided to re-create it as best I could. The food was so good on this trip, Delius and I presented a whole cooking class dedicated to Puget Sound and its culinary marvels after we returned. Of course, with this soup, I had to add my twist, along with what we call our "crack bread" with Herb Butter (page 27)—because it's so addictive; you'll see.

SERVES EIGHT

4 strips bacon
4 tablespoons salted butter
1 large Walla Walla onion
   (or other sweet variety), small dice
2 cloves garlic, minced
1 cup brunoised celery
1½ cups brunoised carrots
2 bay leaves
2 cups diced new red-skin potatoes, skin on,
   washed and dried
3 cups clam broth (fresh or bottled)
4 pounds clams, middle neck or similar size
   of hard-shell clam, rinsed and purged to remove
   sand (how to purge clams is found online)
8 ounces chopped clams, canned or frozen
3 cups heavy cream
1 cup mashed potatoes
¼ cup chopped parsley, for garnish
Kosher salt and freshly ground black pepper, to taste
4 ears pan-charred corn (see below for directions)

In a stockpot over medium-high heat, place whole strips of bacon. Add butter, onion and garlic and sauté just until bacon is crisp.

Add celery, carrots and bay leaves and continue sautéing for 4 minutes. Add potatoes and stir for 2 minutes. Pour in clam broth and stir. Simmer for 10 minutes.

Place clams in pot and cover. Simmer until clams open, then pour in heavy cream. Add chopped clams, then simmer, uncovered, for 5 minutes more. Remove bacon and discard.

Warm mashed potatoes in a microwave and whisk some into soup to thicken, adding more as needed. Taste and adjust seasoning.

Divide among 8 bowls and garnish with parsley and black pepper. Serve with charred corn half and a cocktail fork for the clams.

How to Pan-Char Corn

Husk an ear of corn and break it in half. In a heavy-bottomed skillet, preferably cast iron, place 2 tablespoons of salted butter. When the butter becomes hot, add the cob halves and sear on all sides until all the kernels are charred. Salt and pepper to taste.

Heirloom Tomato Gazpacho
with Shrimp and Avocado Microgreens Salad

Nothing beats a traditional gazpacho. But one year, during the Homestead, Florida, tomato season, which yields all sorts of heirlooms and other interesting varieties, I thought it might be okay to leave out the bread and just let the bright, fresh flavor of our Homestead tomatoes burst through. This soup is light on its own, so serving it with a shrimp and avocado salad turns it into more of a meal.

SERVES EIGHT

Heirloom Tomato Gazpacho

6–8 ripe heirloom tomatoes, diced
6 cloves roasted garlic
2 small cans tomato juice
2 charred red bell peppers, diced, with stems, skins,
    membranes and seeds removed
1 English cucumber, peeled and diced
⅓ cup red onion, minced
1 tablespoon Worcestershire sauce
4 tablespoons sherry vinegar
2 tablespoons lemon juice
¼ cup parsley leaves
4 basil leaves, chiffonaded
⅓ cup olive oil

Shrimp and Avocado Microgreens Salad

1 cup chopped, cooked shrimp
1 cup micro arugula
½ cup brunoised heirloom tomatoes

1 avocado, firm ripe, peeled, pitted and diced
1 teaspoon lemon agrumato oil, plus more for drizzling
Salt and pepper, to taste

Prepare gazpacho

Place all ingredients except the oil in a food processor. Start the processor and slowly add oil. Blend until all ingredients are emulsified with the oil.

Prepare salad

In a small, nonreactive bowl, mix shrimp, tomatoes and arugula and gently toss in avocado, oil, salt and pepper.

Assemble

Divide gazpacho among 8 serving bowls. Garnish with salad and drizzle with additional agrumato oil.

❋ If you're entertaining, as we often do, cut the shrimp salad into tiny brunoise and pour the gazpacho into chilled shot glasses. Serve as gazpacho shooters, with or without a little vodka spike in them.

Italian Escarole Soup
with Meatballs, Ditalini Pasta and Grated Parmigiano-Reggiano

This soup is my personal favorite. It reminds me of my hometown in New Jersey, Berkeley Heights. Exit 135, baby! This was Sunday, for sure. The meatballs had three different meats, and it was imperative that the soup have freshly grated, imported Parmigiano-Reggiano (the real stuff), served with crusty bread. My personal addiction to this soup began with my best friends June and Jean D'Ascoli and their father, Checky. I grew up eating his authentic Italian food. Ever since then, I've been hooked. To this day, when Italian buddies like Tommy Gonnella come to visit us in Miami, the pot of escarole goes on.

SERVES SIX

Veal, Pork and Beef Meatballs
(Makes 30 meatballs)
¼ cup olive oil
1 cup diced onion
¾ cup brunoised celery
¾ cup brunoised carrot
2 tablespoons garlic powder
Pinch of red pepper flakes
2 tablespoons kosher salt
2 large eggs
½ cup heavy cream
¾ cup Quaker Quick Oats
½ cup freshly grated Parmigiano-Reggiano
½ cup chopped Italian parsley
½ pound ground beef
½ pound ground veal
½ pound ground pork

Escarole Soup
(Makes 6 quarts)
3 cups cooked ditalini pasta
⅓ cup olive oil
8 cloves garlic, peeled, smashed
   and coarsely chopped
1 cup diced carrots
1½ cups diced celery
¾ cup small-diced fennel bulb
12 large basil leaves
4 quarts homemade chicken stock
2 cups vine-ripe Roma tomatoes, diced
2 heads escarole, thoroughly cleaned
   and coarsely chopped
12 ounces cooked cannellini beans (or canned)
Grated Parmigiano-Reggiano, for garnish
Red pepper flakes, for garnish

continued on page 26

continued from page 24

Prepare meatballs

In a skillet, heat olive oil and sauté onion, celery and carrot until tender. Add garlic powder, red pepper flakes and salt. Remove from heat and place on a tray in the refrigerator to cool.

Preheat oven to 375°F.

In a bowl, whisk eggs, heavy cream, oats, Parmigiano-Reggiano and parsley. Remove sautéed vegetable mixture from refrigerator and add to bowl. Combine thoroughly.

Put on gloves, add meats and gently hand-mix all ingredients. Form into 1-ounce balls and place on baking sheets. Bake in the oven for about 10 minutes. Make sure when you add the meatballs to the soup, you scrape all the juice and meaty bits into the pot of soup from the baking tray.

Prepare escarole soup

Cook pasta according to box's instructions and set aside.

In a stockpot over medium-high heat, place olive oil, garlic and onion and sauté until tender.

Add carrots, celery, fennel and basil. Stir for 2 to 3 minutes. Add chicken stock and bring to a boil. Once boiling, reduce to a low simmer and add the beans.

Add tomatoes, escarole and par-cooked meatballs. Simmer until meatballs are cooked through. Add the pasta and serve with grated Parmigiano-Reggiano and red pepper flakes.

 This soup is also wonderful when prepared with Italian sausage instead of, or in addition to, meatballs.

Clarified Butter

2 pounds (8 sticks) salted butter

Heat butter in a pot over medium heat. As it begins to melt and bubble, skim off foam that forms on the top using a small ladle. Discard into a heatproof container. Continue doing this skimming until you are left with a clear butter.

Remove from stove and carefully pour clear butter into a clean heatproof container. Avoid stirring up any milk solids that have dropped to the bottom of the pot while clarifying. These should be left behind and discarded.

Makes about 3 cups

✳ If I am going to make clarified butter, I always make more than I need and store it in deli cups in my refrigerator for whenever I need it. I use clarified butter to pan-sear fish, poultry and meats before finishing them in the oven to give them those crisp, golden-brown edges. Clarified butter also makes a better hollandaise sauce that won't break.

Herb Butter

2 pounds (8 sticks) salted butter, room temperature
2–3 cloves garlic, minced
½ cup finely chopped Italian parsley leaves
1 bunch finely chopped scallions, green parts only
1 bunch or box chives, finely chopped
Salt and pepper, to taste

In a stainless-steel or glass bowl, place softened butter. Combine all ingredients well. The butter is ready to use immediately.

Store in an airtight container in the refrigerator. Butter will keep in the

Butters

refrigerator for about 2 months, and longer in the freezer.

Makes a little more than 2 pounds

✳ This butter is so addictive, we affectionately call it "crack butter" in our restaurants. The good news is, aside from the fat content, it's not really harmful to your health. The butter enhances everything from bread to vegetables, starches to steak. Serve on toasted baguette slices with Red Stripe Mediterranean Mussels (page 52); the Caribbean Steamed Fish One Pot (page 126); or any of the soups in this chapter.

Ginger-Almond Butter

3 cups skin-on almonds
1 tablespoon sea salt
1 tablespoon ground ginger
2 tablespoons honey

In a food processor, place almonds, sea salt and ginger. Turn machine on and pulse. After a few minutes, mixture will become crumbly, then finely ground. Then, as oils are released, it will get lumpy. At this point, stop machine and scrape down sides. It should take about 5 minutes to get to this stage.

Add honey and continue processing. As oils are released it should become the texture of peanut butter, about another 5 minutes. Once creamy, stop and scrape into a Mason jar.

Store in the refrigerator for up to 2 months.

Makes about 1½ cups

✳ Almond butter is excellent as a quick remedy to kill hunger pangs. Try to incorporate 1 tablespoon daily to maintain your diet. It is also excellent with apple slices, pancakes or oatmeal. Use as a spread with the Grilled Nectarine, Prosciutto, Arugula and Feta Cheese sandwich (page 114) or as a condiment in a recipe of your choice.

Jamaican Red Pea Soup

When I was nine months pregnant with my first son, I met this six-foot-tall Chinese Jamaican woman. Her name was Rosalie Day. She was dating a crazy friend of my husband at the time. Little did I know what that introduction would have in store for me and my life's journey through Jamaica, its culture, my past life, its food . . . oh yes, and its men! It's also important to mention Iris Day, Rosalie's mother. She was a trip. That woman could cook, and it was through her that I began learning about my Jamaican "culinary roots." Over the years, the Day family became my dearest friends, and Iris let me keep this recipe—along with many more you will see throughout this book. This is her soup, ramped up with my twist.

SERVES SIX

3 cups kidney beans, dried or canned

¼ cup of extra-virgin coconut oil

2 regular onions, diced (about 3 cups)

2 cloves garlic, chopped

4–6 quarts water or chicken stock

1 smoked ham hock

1 tablespoon whole Jamaican allspice

3 tablespoons dried thyme

1½ pounds potatoes, diced fine

1½ pounds Jamaican yellow yam or malanga,
   peeled and diced

1 cup diced carrots

2 scallions, chopped

1 Scotch bonnet chili pepper

1 tablespoon kosher salt

1 teaspoon freshly ground black pepper

1 can coconut milk

If you are using dried kidney beans, then soak them in water overnight.

In a stockpot, heat coconut oil and sauté onions and garlic.

Place beans (including the water they were soaked in) in a large saucepan and add more water or chicken stock to make a total of 6 quarts. Add ham hock, allspice and thyme. Bring to a boil, then reduce to a simmer, uncovered, until fork-tender, about 1 hour. Add diced potatoes, yam, carrots and scallions into the pot. Float the whole Scotch bonnet in the soup, taking care not to burst it.

Add salt, pepper and coconut milk and allow to simmer until vegetables are tender, about 20 minutes. Remove Scotch bonnet. If you would like the soup spicy, split pepper open, remove seeds, chop the flesh and return to soup.

❋ Red peas are not really peas. They are red kidney beans. Jamaicans always refer to beans as peas, as in "Jamaican rice 'n' peas." If you would like to make a red pea bisque, omit the Jamaican yam and potatoes and blend after cooking.

Loaded Baked Potato Bisque

with Vande Rose Farms Bacon Lardoons and Cabot Clothbound Cheddar in Russet Cups

This bisque is definitely a bowl of comfort on a chilly day. In it, I use Vande Rose Farms bacon, which is made from Duroc pork that's rubbed with brown sugar before it's smoked over applewood; I crave the fruity taste and noticeable smoke. If you prefer lighter smoke, you could look for Nodine's bacon, also excellent. (Both can be purchased online.) As for the cheese, there are so many fantastic artisanal makers now. I happen to like Jasper Hill Farm, whose 10-month-aged Cabot clothbound cheddar pairs terrifically with this soup. Pour this soup in a mug, add some chopped green onion, freshly cracked black pepper and sour cream, then curl up on the couch and enjoy. Or if you have guests to impress, use the hollowed-out Russet potato skins as edible "mugs" and serve along with a glass of fine Chardonnay.

SERVES EIGHT

Loaded Baked Potato Bisque

8 large Idaho potatoes, washed and dried
1½ cups cooked potato, no skin
1 tablespoon olive oil
Salt, to taste
1 stick salted butter
4 cloves garlic, smashed with flat side of knife
2½ cups sliced leeks, white parts only
1 cup sliced onion
4 cups chicken stock
¼ cup fresh thyme leaves
2 cups heavy cream
½ teaspoon freshly grated nutmeg
Black pepper, to taste

Vande Rose Farms Bacon Lardoons and Cabot Clothbound Cheddar

1 cup Vande Rose Farms bacon lardoons
2 cups grated Cabot Clothbound Cheddar
  by Jasper Hill Farm
1 bunch scallions, green parts only, sliced thin
8 rounded tablespoons sour cream
¼ cup finely chopped parsley
¼ cup finely chopped chives

continued on page 32

continued from page 30

Prepare loaded baked potato bisque

After washing and drying potatoes, slice a small sliver off the potato lengthwise so it will lie flat on a plate. Then flip it over and remove about a ¼-inch-thick piece off the other side. Holding the potato firmly in one hand, begin digging out the insides with a melon baller or tablespoon, forming a potato bowl with an equal thickness on the inside, about ¼ inch. (Save potato insides to cook and add to the bisque later.)

Preheat oven to 400°F. Rub the potato bowls with olive oil and sprinkle with salt. Bake them, opening side down, for about 15 minutes or until fork-tender.

Meanwhile, prepare the lardoons and cheddar mixture. Cook bacon lardoons until crispy. Combine all ingredients in a bowl and reserve for garnish.

As the hollowed out potatoes are roasting in the oven, place an 8-quart stock pot on medium-high heat. Melt butter and begin sauteeing the leeks, onions and garlic. When tender, add the scooped out potato insides and sauté for about 5 minutes. Add chicken stock, thyme, nutmeg, salt and pepper. Bring to a simmer, then add the cooked potatoes and heavy cream and stir. Simmer for an additional 5 to 10 minutes. Then blend to a smooth bisque. Season with salt and pepper to taste.

Using a hand-held or traditional blender, blend bisque until smooth (the latter works best to produce a smooth bisque). While still hot, pour bisque into hollowed-out potato skins. Top with reserved garnish.

Roasted Tomato-Kaffir Lime Leaf Bisque
with Goat Cheese Ice

This soup requires the addition of fragrant kaffir lime leaves. You can order them online, either from Thai Kitchen in packaged form or fresh from Thai Table. I have my own tree, which is fortunate for me, because kaffir lime leaves can be very expensive. There really is no substitute for them, although you could try a combination of lemongrass and fresh lemon juice. I assure you, though, it is not the same. At any rate, whenever I plan to serve this soup at any of our locations, we have a list of customers to call so they can plan a trip to the restaurant. When I'm not in town, Chef Andy Harrinanan is the only one who can make it, and my daughter is the official taste-tester for this soup, simply because, as with many patrons, it's her favorite.

SERVES EIGHT TO TEN

1 (4-ounce) log goat cheese, room temperature
1 (4-ounce) log goat cheese, frozen
4 quarts vine-ripe tomatoes (about 4 pounds)
1 tablespoon olive oil
Kosher salt and freshly ground black pepper, to taste
1 stick salted butter
2 cups sliced leeks, white parts only
1 quart sliced onions
¼ cup chopped garlic
8 kaffir lime leaves
1 teaspoon freshly toasted and ground cumin
1 tablespoon freshly toasted and ground coriander
2 cups chicken stock
2 cups heavy cream

Place log of goat cheese in the freezer. Preheat oven to 375°F.

Core tomatoes, discarding as many seeds as possible without crushing the fruit. Dry cored tomatoes with paper towels, then lightly rub with olive oil. Sprinkle with salt and pepper, place on a baking sheet, and roast for 10 minutes or until soft.

Meanwhile, in a stockpot, melt butter. Add leeks, onions and garlic and slowly caramelize until soft and slightly golden in color.

Add kaffir lime leaves, cumin, coriander and chicken stock and season to taste. Cook at a simmer for 5 minutes.

Remove tomatoes from oven and, when cool enough to handle, shake out remaining seeds. Add tomatoes to the stock and stir. While continuously stirring, add heavy cream and remaining log goat cheese. Simmer for 5 minutes more.

In a blender, process soup until smooth. Pass mixture through a China cap to remove any chunks. Taste for seasoning and adjust as necessary.

Pour into soup bowls. Remove goat cheese from freezer and shave with a microplane for the "ice" garnish. Serve immediately.

Traditional "Peppa" Pot Soup

with Salt Beef and Stewed-Down Pig's Tail and Herbed Spinners

I will never forget the first time I tasted *peppa* (pepper) pot soup. I was dating a Jamaican man I had met in Miami named Charles Hutson. He took me on a vacation to meet his mother and to see Jamaica for the first time. His mom's driver, Mr. Taylor, picked us up at the airport, and up into the Blue Mountains we went. The road there was filled with street vendors. The smell of wood, coal, great food and *ganja* (marijuana) permeated the clear mountain air. Each vendor called out for us to "cum cum, nyam pon dis," which means "Come eat this." Somehow, I felt like I had been there before. Somehow, I understood the language, the flavors, the smells and the culture. Of course, most people that knew me said what I understood was the Red Stripe, the ganja and the great food. Anyway, whether or not I'd had it in a past life, the pepper pot in this life was amazing. Here is my version. Oh, and yes—Charles Hutson became my second husband, father of my son Christian and daughter, Ashley.

SERVES SIX

Peppa Pot Soup

1 pound salt (corned) beef, cut into 2-inch strips

1 pound brined pig's tail, chopped at the joints
  into pieces 1 to 1½ inches long

7 quarts fresh water

½ stick salted butter

2 cups diced onions

6 cloves garlic, chopped

10 allspice berries

1 Scotch bonnet chili pepper

½ cup loosely packed, fresh thyme leaves

10 ounces fresh coconut milk
  (plus more if broth becomes too salty)

12 okra, sliced horizontally

2 cups medium-dice carrots

2 cups 1-inch-cubed Russet potatoes

2 cups 1-inch-cubed Jamaican yellow yam

1½ cups diced tomatoes

2 cups 1-inch-cubed malanga

1 pound callaloo, washed, leaves separated
  from stems, chopped

Herbed Spinners

In a container, place salt beef and pig's tail and cover with cold water, about 2 quarts. You want them to soak in the water while you prepare the remaining ingredients to remove some of the salt from the meats.

In a stockpot over medium-high heat, melt butter and begin to sauté onions, garlic and allspice. After

continued on page 38

continued from page 36

1 or 2 minutes, add chili pepper and continue to sauté, taking care not to break it.

When onions are almost tender, drain and discard water from the meats, then cut up beef into bite-size pieces. Discard any large pieces of fat.

Add both beef and pig's tail to the onion mixture and cover with remaining 5 quarts water. Bring to a boil and add coconut milk. Reduce heat to a steady simmer and add ¼ cup thyme. Simmer for at least 45 to 60 minutes, until meats are tender.

Once tender, check to see if the stock has become too salty. If it has, slowly add more water until desired flavor has been achieved. At this point you can also add more coconut milk, if desired, to alleviate salt and add richness.

Now add okra, carrots, potatoes, yam and tomatoes. Simmer for 10 minutes more.

Add malanga and callaloo and cook for 10 minutes or until all vegetables are fork-tender. Add spinners (see recipe at right for instructions) and cook for 5 minutes more.

Serve hot in soup bowls, making sure everyone gets some spinners. This is one of those soups that gets better over time, so you can prepare it in advance and reheat it before serving.

Makes 8 quarts

Herbed Spinners

1 cup all-purpose flour
1 tablespoon kosher salt
1 teaspoon chopped fresh thyme leaves
1 teaspoon chopped fresh parsley
½ cup cold water (plus a little more if needed)

In a small bowl, place flour, salt and herbs and combine well. Slowly add water, mixing with your hands. The dough should be firm and hold together.

Break off small pieces and roll between fingers of both hands in a spinning motion. Each spinner should be about 1½ inches long.

Spin them into the simmering pot of soup, one by one. Although you might be tempted to spin them onto a paper towel or plate and add them all at once, they tend to stick to surfaces. This is why cooks spin them right into a pot.

❋ This soup takes some dedicated effort to make, but it's well worth the comfort in the end. It gets easier each time you make it.

However, it can be difficult to find several of these ingredients unless you have Caribbean markets nearby. If you don't, you can make the following substitutions: smoked ham hock for pig's tail; brined corned beef for salt beef; canned coconut milk for fresh coconut milk; kale or spinach for fresh callaloo. Jamaican yellow yam can be very bitter, so if you find it, you should have a knowledgeable store clerk pick it out for you. If you can't find it, South American white yam or ñame could be substituted as well.

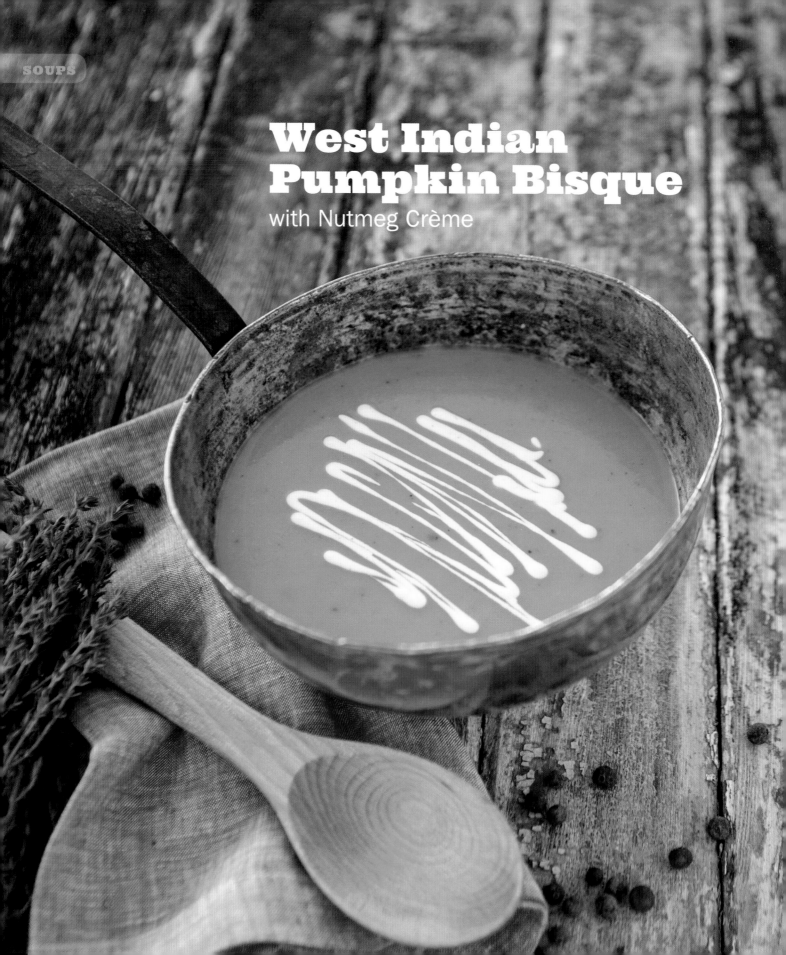

West Indian Pumpkin Bisque

with Nutmeg Crème

The soup is fast to make, delicious to eat and perfect to serve for fall and winter holidays. As smooth and rich as this soup is, no cream or roux is added. It is just fresh vegetables and uses onions as the thickener, making it gluten free and almost dairy free. (To keep it lightweight, leave out the crème garnish.) It might be difficult to get calabaza, a Caribbean pumpkin, in the northeast or Midwest, so perhaps kabocha squash is easier to find than our tropical variety.

SERVES TWELVE

West Indian Pumpkin Bisque

¼ cup Herb Butter (page 27)

1 large Vidalia or yellow onion, sliced

4 cloves garlic, chopped

1 cup sliced carrots

1 smoked ham hock (you can substitute
  3 strips of smoked bacon)

1 Scotch bonnet chili pepper

¼ cup fresh thyme leaves

3 pounds calabaza, seeded, peeled and diced

8 allspice berries

2 quarts chicken stock (plus 2 cups more if soup
  is too thick after blending)

Salt and pepper, to taste

In a large stockpot over medium heat, place butter, onion, garlic and carrots and sauté until caramelized, being careful not to burn.

Add ham hock, chili pepper and thyme and cook, stirring, for 2 to 3 minutes. Add calabaza, allspice and chicken stock. Bring to a boil, then lower heat and simmer for 45 minutes, uncovered, or until all vegetables are cooked through.

Remove from heat and let cool for about 15 minutes. Remove Scotch bonnet and ham hock and set aside. If desired, remove seeds from pepper, chop up flesh and add back to the soup for spice. When ham hock is cool enough to handle, pick the meat to use in addition to the créme garnish.

Place soup in a blender and blend until smooth. Season with salt and pepper to taste, and serve. Garnish with Nutmeg Crème (recipe below).

Makes 4 quarts

Nutmeg Crème

1 cup sour cream

¼ cup heavy cream

1 tablespoon freshly grated nutmeg

1 teaspoon kosher salt

Place all ingredients in a bowl and whisk until smooth.

Makes 1¼ cups

 To make the soup vegetarian, replace the chicken stock with vegetable stock and leave out the ham hock.

When Blending Hot Soup

Use a cloth to remove the center piece from the top of the blender cover and pulse the blender, releasing the steam so that you do not accidentally explode the apparatus. Once steam escapes, full speed ahead!

CHAPTER 2

APPETI

Many of the appetizer recipes I have included in this chapter are also wonderful when served as entrées. Often, when I run them on the menu at any of our restaurants, patrons order the Red Stripe Mediterranean Mussels (page 52), for instance, with a side of rice and asparagus, and make a light meal out of it. For lunch, the West Indian Curried Crab Cake (page 60) is a natural when paired with the Norma's Terrace Salad (page 82). Versatility is the key here. However you choose to pair them, or in whatever order you like to cook and consume them, is up to you.

ZERS

Braised Octopus Tiradito

with Yuzu Ponzu, Jalapeños
and Asian Napa Cabbage Salad with
Orange-Ginger Vinaigrette

Many of the recipes I have put together over the years have been motivated by my travels or by the various chefs and employees I have had in my restaurants. This one was inspired by a combination of both place and personality—a trip to Tokyo and a chef de cuisine, Ilde Ferrer, who taught me how to put the octopus together like this and slice it in this fantastic design. It's light, refreshing and gorgeous to look at, producing that "Wow" effect that every chef and home cook hopes to achieve. You must have a mandoline or sharp meat slicer to create this dish presentation.

SERVES SIX

Braised Octopus Tiradito

2 (2½-pound) whole octopuses,
    cleaned, beaks removed
1 cup dry white wine
½ cup black peppercorns
10 cloves garlic, smashed with flat side of knife
1 large white onion, roughly chopped
1 fennel bulb, plus fronds, roughly chopped
2 lemons, cut in half
1 wine-bottle cork

Yuzu Ponzu

¼ cup freshly squeezed orange juice
½ cup yuzu
3 tablespoons rice vinegar
3 tablespoons mirin
¼ cup soy sauce
2 tablespoons brown sugar
½ cup bonito flakes

Asian Napa Cabbage Salad

2 cups shaved Napa cabbage (do this on a mandoline)
½ cup julienned red bell peppers
½ cup julienned yellow bell peppers
3 jalapeño peppers, seeded, sliced thin
3 scallions, green parts only, sliced
¼ pound snow peas, sliced thin on a bias

Orange-Ginger Vinaigrette

¼ cup chopped roasted garlic
1 roasted shallot, chopped
1 teaspoon freshly grated ginger
1 teaspoon onion powder
1 teaspoon garlic powder
1 teaspoon ground ginger powder
½ cup freshly squeezed orange juice
½ cup orange marmalade
1 tablespoon kosher salt
½ tablespoon ground, toasted coriander
¼ cup honey
1 tablespoon sugar
¾ cup apple cider vinegar
1¾ cups canola-vegetable oil blend

Prepare octopus tiradito

In a large pot, place all ingredients, including the cork, and cover with room-temperature water by 1 inch. Place over high heat, bring liquid to a boil, then reduce to a simmer. Cover with a lid and cook for 45 to 90 minutes, until tender. (The large difference in time depends on whether or not your octopuses have been pre-tenderized. See note.) The octopuses are tender enough when easily pierced with a fork. Drain and let cool to room temperature.

continued on page 46

continued from page 45

When octopuses are still warm but cool enough to touch, take a sturdy paper towel and wipe the tentacles to remove some of the red gelatin that forms during cooking. Remove the heads and discard (there really is not that much meat in an octopus head).

Now take both octopuses and entwine the tentacles from one into the other as if you were clasping your hands together. Then place the combined octopus in plastic wrap and roll it up. Twist the ends together so you get a nice tight roll. Poke a couple of holes in the wrap with a toothpick and twist again to release some air and juices. Wrap a second time with plastic and twist again. Place the roll in the freezer so it will be easy to slice.

Once frozen solid, the octopus can be easily sliced on a mandoline or meat slicer. Remove wrap from where you want to slice. Hold firmly on the other end and press down hard. Make about 6 slices and lay out flat in a pattern on a salad plate, covering the bottom in a nice design. Prepare 5 more plates this way. Rewrap the remaining log and return to the freezer. It will keep for up to 1 month.

❋ **Most fishmongers have tumbled or "tenderized" octopus already before you purchase it. You will also want to ask if they have cleaned the ink sac and removed the beak for you. As for the cork thing, some swear by it for tenderizing. I think it's a myth, but it certainly strikes up a conversation. At any rate, it's a good excuse for drinking a bottle of wine with friends while you prepare the dish!**

Prepare yuzu ponzu

In a container, whisk all ingredients together. Let sit for about 2 hours. Strain. Use immediately, or refrigerate for future use; it will keep for about 1 week.

Makes about 1½ cups

Prepare cabbage salad

In a large stainless-steel bowl, combine all ingredients and toss thoroughly.

Prepare orange-ginger vinaigrette

In a blender, place all ingredients except the oil. Blend on low speed until mixed. While blender is mixing, slowly drizzle in oil until fully incorporated.

Makes 1 quart

Assemble

Add the vinaigrette to the cabbage salad. Toss to coat. Spoon about 4 tablespoons yuzu ponzu over the sliced octopus on each plate. Then place the Asian Napa cabbage salad in the center of each plate and serve with chopsticks for an Asian touch.

Cuban-Style Bacalao Fritters à la Cat Cay

with Roasted Garlic and Scotch Bonnet Aioli

We have made friends with some wonderful people at Ortanique. Meeting these people and their families has opened many doors for travel, fun and new recipes. Thanks to some of these friends, in particular the Gomez and Cabrerizo families, we've been able to visit Cat Cay, a small private island in the Bahamas, where many Miamians have their vacation homes. Delius and I spent a fantastic July 4th weekend there one year cooking, drinking unbelievable wines, yo-yo fishing (a technique where you laboriously haul in ridiculously large fish by hand-winding a spool of fishing line with a hook and bait on the end), and embracing the wonderful Cuban culture—in particular, the Gomez and Cabrerizo families. Feeling like one of the family, I borrowed this recipe from matriarch Miriam Gomez. Then I adapted it by adding a few more ingredients, pairing it with a garlic and Scotch bonnet aioli, and placed it on the Ortanique menu. This recipe needs to be started 24 hours in advance in order for the salt cod to be soaked.

MAKES ABOUT 30 FRITTERS

Cuban-Style Bacalao Fritters à la Cat Cay

1 pound salt cod, soaked in cold water overnight

2 cups diced yellow onion

1 large bunch Italian parsley, washed and picked

1–2 tablespoons seeded and chopped Scotch bonnet chili peppers

3 tablespoons kosher salt

3 tablespoons baking powder

4 cups cold, fresh water

4 cups all-purpose flour

Vegetable or peanut oil for frying, enough to cover

Roasted Garlic and Scotch Bonnet Aioli (page 109)

Prepare bacalao fritters

The day before you want to make this recipe, rinse salt cod under cold water. Tear into large strips and place in a container. Cover with cold water and let soak, refrigerated, overnight.

Remove container from refrigerator and pour out soaking water. Using a fork, shred fish. Then cut with a knife, making sure there are no stringy pieces left. Place in a stainless-steel bowl and set aside.

In a Robot Coupe, place onion, parsley and Scotch bonnet. Pulse about 12 times.

continued on page 50

continued from page 48

Add parsley mixture, salt, baking powder and the fresh water to the fish and mix by hand.

Still mixing by hand, gently incorporate flour.

In a skillet, place oil over medium-high heat. Oil is ready for frying when a cube of white bread is placed in the oil and turns golden brown or the oil hits about 325°F on a candy thermometer. Once oil is ready, drop in batter in 1-ounce scoops (about 1 tablespoon). Repeat a few times; do not overcrowd the pan. Oil should cover the batter. Fry each batch, turning a few times with a metal slotted spoon, until golden brown

and cooked through. Remove with slotted spoon and drain on paper towels.

Serve hot with the aioli.

✳ I prefer to use peanut oil for frying when allergies aren't an issue, but vegetable oil works as well.

Prepare aioli

In a blender, place all ingredients except the oil. While blending, slowly add oil until emulsified. Do not over blend.

Makes 4 cups

Rémoulade

2 cups Basic Aioli (page 108)

2 hard-boiled egg yolks

2 teaspoons minced fresh garlic

4 tablespoons minced yellow onion

2 tablespoons horseradish

3 tablespoons Creole mustard

2 tablespoons ketchup

¼ cup brunoised celery

¼ cup freshly squeezed lemon juice

½ cup chopped scallions,
   green parts only

¼ cup chopped parsley

Salt and pepper, to taste

¼ cup olive oil

Condiments

Prepare aioli and set aside.

Except olive oil, add each remaining ingredient in the order listed to the bowl of a food processor while motor is running. Once seasoned, drizzle in oil until incorporated and mixture has emulsified.

Stop machine and scrape mixture into a bowl. Fold in aioli.

Store refrigerated in an airtight container for up to 1½ weeks.

Makes 2½ cups

✱ This recipe can take the place of ordinary mayonnaise on any sandwich. I mix it in with tuna in the Open-Faced Cherry Wood-Smoked Tuna Salad (page 120).

Cilantro Crema

1 cup sour cream

1 bunch cilantro,
   cleaned and chopped

Juice of 1 lime

½ tablespoon kosher salt

In a nonreactive stainless-steel bowl, whisk all ingredients together.

Makes 1 cup

✱ The Cilantro Crema is an excellent condiment for any Mexican, Southwestern or spice-heavy recipe. I use it to complement the Marinated Mahi-Mahi in Breadfruit Taco Shells with Pico de Gallo (page 112) as well as the Cumin- and Coriander-Dusted Mahi-Mahi with Eggplant and Vine-Ripe Tomato Sauté, Slivered Garlic and Sambal Pepper Sauce (page 128). It would also be deliciously over-the-top with my Queso Blanco-Stuffed Chicken Breast with Fire-Roasted Salsa Verde (page 176).

Local Mango Chimichurri

1 cup finely chopped cilantro

1 cup chopped parsley, no stems

1 bunch scallions,
   green parts only, chopped fine

2 cloves fresh garlic, minced

¼ cup lime juice

½ cup orange juice

½ cup olive oil

½ cup vegetable oil

2 tablespoons red wine vinegar

Pinch of cayenne pepper

½ teaspoon red pepper flakes

⅔ cup brunoised ripe mango

½ cup unsweetened mango puree
   (if you can't do it fresh,
   Boiron is an unsweetened brand)

2 tablespoons sugar

1 tablespoon kosher salt

In a nonreactive bowl, whisk all ingredients together for about 1 minute.

Place ¼ mixture in a blender and purée. Then combine in bowl with remaining mixture.

Makes about 3 cups

✱ This chimichurri is magnificent when brushed on the Certified Angus Beef Grilled Flat Iron Steak (page 188), but don't let that stop you from also using it with grilled vegetables.

Red Stripe Mediterranean Mussels

in a Spicy Red Stripe Broth of Shallots, Tomatoes, Scallions, Thyme, Scotch Bonnet, and Red and Yellow Peppers, with Toasted Herb Butter Garlic Bread

I discovered Mediterranean mussels back when we had our first restaurant, Norma's on the Beach. We used a very large, meaty mussel that was farmed in the Santa Barbara Basin. In my opinion, this variety is far better than the Prince Edward Island mussels, which are a smaller blue mussel with a little less of that briny seafood flavor. I steamed them in a good white wine with lots of Jamaican thyme and fresh Scotch bonnet peppers. They were so tasty. One night, this badass line cook that I had, Charlie McKibben, was by himself on the line, being himself, and a mussel order came in. There was no wine in sight, just a bottle of Red Stripe. So he popped it open with his tongs, poured it in the mussels with everything else, and that was all she wrote. The Red Stripe mussels were born. Thank you, Charlie!

SERVES EIGHT

Red Stripe Mediterranean Mussels and Spicy Broth

4 tablespoons Herb Butter (page 27), divided
3 large shallots, sliced thin on mandoline
1 cup fine-dice red and yellow bell peppers
1 bunch fresh thyme, leaves picked, stems discarded
48 Mediterranean mussels, washed and debearded
8 ounces clam or mussel broth
24 ounces Red Stripe beer
1½ cups diced tomatoes
1 teaspoon Scotch bonnet hot sauce (optional)
⅓ cup sliced scallions
Kosher salt, to taste or about 1 tablespoon

Toasted Herb Butter Garlic Bread

1 French baguette, sliced into 16–20 portions
8 tablespoons Herb Butter (page 27)

Prepare mussels and broth

Heat a sauté pan, add 2 tablespoons butter and sauté shallots for 2 minutes.

Add peppers, thyme, mussels, clam broth and beer. Cover and cook until mussels open.

Add tomatoes, hot sauce, scallions and remaining butter. Simmer until butter is emulsified. Season with salt to taste.

❋ Be judicious with the hot sauce. The mussels should be flavorful, not overly spicy. Also, if there is any broth left over, save it. It's perfect for the next day. Just add some sautéed garlic shrimp and serve it over any kind of pasta for a quick and light meal.

Prepare garlic bread

Slather each slice of baguette with Herb Butter. Place on a cookie sheet and cook under a broiler until golden brown.

Plate mussels in soup bowls. Serve steaming hot with the buttered garlic bread.

Society Island Tuna Tartare

with Vanilla-Scented Pineapple, Coconut,
Lemongrass and Kaffir Lime Sauce and Toasted Coconut Chips

Delius had always wanted to go to Bora Bora. His desire was reinforced by a number of coincidences: a brochure sent to us from Radisson cruises for a voyage to Bora Bora aboard the *Paul Gauguin;* a travel show he randomly tuned in to that was highlighting the Cook Islands; a magazine that magically opened to a feature on Bora Bora. Lucky for me, my 40th birthday was coming up, so Delius obeyed the signs and booked us a trip there. It was an amazing journey, filled with welcoming people and gorgeous scenery. Interestingly, there wasn't a whole lot of culinary diversity, but what the islanders did have was fresh tuna, and plenty of it. They also harvest vanilla, and I actually conceived this dish during a visit to a vanilla bean plantation.

SERVES SIX TO EIGHT

Coconut, Lemongrass and Kaffir Lime Sauce

4 tablespoons vegetable oil

1 cup thinly sliced shallots

7 cloves garlic, smashed with flat side of knife

1 large stalk lemongrass, chopped

8 kaffir lime leaves, chopped

4 tablespoons fresh ginger juice

4 tablespoons fish sauce

1 cup white wine

½ cup rice vinegar

½ cup clam stock

1 tablespoon lemon zest

2 cans coconut milk

Society Island Tuna Tartare

1 cup pineapple, brunoised

½ fresh vanilla bean, scraped and seeded,
   shell reserved for another use

1 pound sushi-grade tuna,
   diced into pinky-nail-size cubes

¼ cup brunoised red onion

¼ cup brunoised European cucumber, seeded, skin on

1 tablespoon sambal sauce

½–¾ cup Coconut, Lemongrass
   and Kaffir Lime Sauce

1 cup fresh Coconut Chips (recipe below,
   or substitute your favorite chip)

continued on page 56

continued from page 54
Coconut Chips

1 whole coconut
2 tablespoons virgin coconut oil
Sea salt, to taste

Prepare sauce

Heat a saucepot over medium and add oil, shallots and garlic. Sauté until soft.

Add lemongrass and kaffir lime leaves. Sauté for about 4 minutes.

Add ginger juice, fish sauce and wine and reduce. Add vinegar, clam stock, lemon zest and coconut milk and bring to a boil, cooking, uncovered, until reduced by half.

Remove from heat. Pour into a blender and carefully blend.

Strain through a chinois into a container and set in an ice bath to cool.

Makes about 1 cup

Prepare tuna tartare

In a small bowl, toss pineapple with the scraped insides of the vanilla bean. Set aside.

In a stainless-steel bowl, place tuna, red onion and cucumber. Mix gently. Add pineapple, sambal and ½ cup lime sauce. Toss. If it seems too dry, add a bit more lime sauce; if you like more spice, add more sambal. Toss again to mix thoroughly.

Prepare coconut chips

Preheat oven to 350°F.

Remove coconut from its shell by cracking it with a mallet (remember it has liquid inside so do this over a pan; reserve the liquid to drink or for another recipe).

Using a vegetable peeler, make coconut shavings. Place on a cookie sheet. Drizzle with coconut oil and sprinkle with salt. Place in oven and lightly toast for about 5 minutes.

Serve tartare molded on small plates with garnishes of coconut chips.

Traditional "Twisted" Bahamian Conch Ceviche

with Tomatoes, Sour Orange, Mango, Ginger, and Red, Yellow, Green and Scotch Bonnet Peppers

In my early days of being a captain on a fishing boat out of Miami, I used to regularly take charters through the Florida Keys and over to the Bahamian island of Bimini. There, we stopped at Brown's Marina, where a young Bahamian boy taught me how to pull conch from the shell and clean it. When you do this, a clear piece called the pistol, which looks like a small piece of cooked vermicelli, comes out of the conch. The Bahamians believe this is the conch's "Viagra." The young boy would fold his arms and tell me, smiling, that the pistol makes men "strong and last a long time." Over on Harbour Island, it makes me laugh every time to see the conch men entertain the tourists and convince the men to eat that limp noodle, no pun intended, to keep them strong for their ladies. Of course, it should be noted that the pistol has no real flavor—and no real effect, either.

SERVES EIGHT

1 pound conch, orange flaps removed and diced
2 cups diced vine-ripe tomatoes
½ cup brunoised red onion
1 green bell pepper, seeded and diced
1 Scotch bonnet chili pepper, seeded and minced
2 tablespoons sugar
1 firm, ripe avocado, peeled, pitted and diced (optional)
1 ripe mango, peeled, pitted and diced (optional)
6 key limes
1 sour orange
Kosher salt and black pepper, to taste

In a nonreactive stainless-steel bowl, place conch, tomatoes, onion, peppers and sugar. Add one or both optional ingredients. Squeeze key limes and sour orange over the ingredients. Season with salt and pepper and toss. Taste and reseason if necessary, adding more sugar to reduce tartness. Serve immediately at room temperature.

＊ Take time to seek out the highest-quality conch available. It is okay to buy frozen product but it should be from the Turks and Caicos Islands, Bahamas, or Belize or Honduras. It should be very white in color and have almost a sweet smell, similar to that of a fresh scallop.

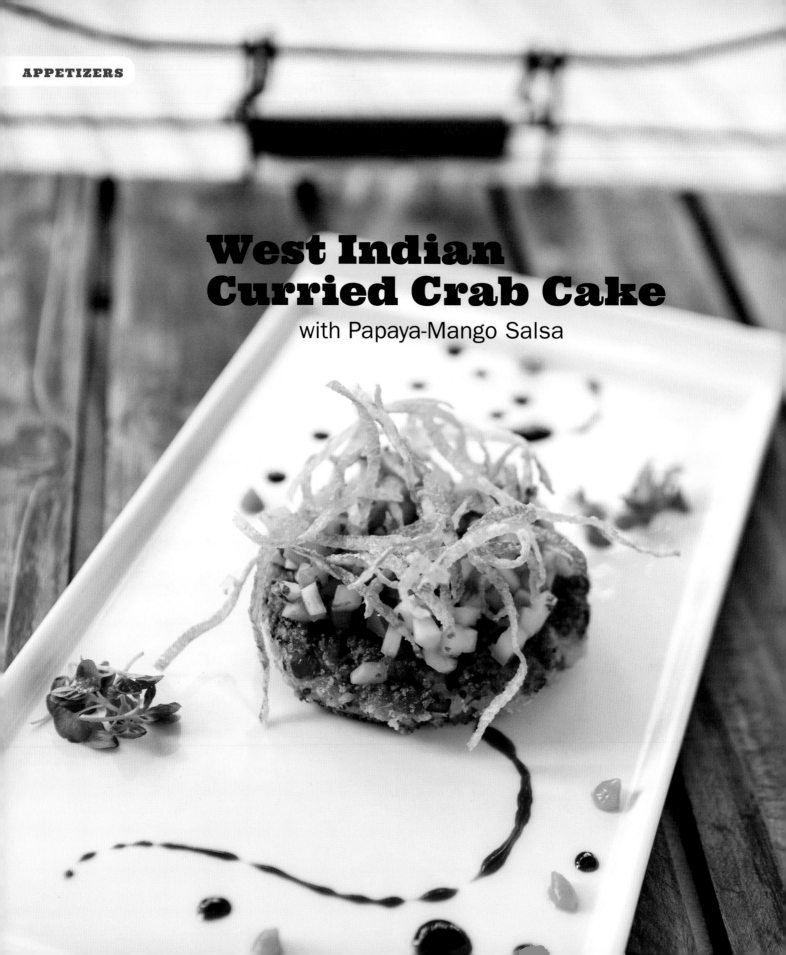

West Indian Curried Crab Cake

with Papaya-Mango Salsa

Growing up in the southern Northeast, I ate a good number of mid-Atlantic-style crab cakes. Although delicious, that Old Bay flavor and bready texture got tiresome. So I spiked up this recipe with a toasted curry blend instead, then balanced out the spices with fresh fruit salsa. Mango season in Miami—May through September—is the best time to make this dish.

SERVES EIGHT

West Indian Curried Crab Cake

3 eggs
½ cup mayonnaise
1 tablespoon whole-grain mustard
1 tablespoon Worcestershire sauce
2 tablespoons Madras curry powder
   (substitute Javin or other high-quality curry powder)
2 scallions, chopped, green parts only
¼ cup fine-dice red bell pepper
¼ cup fine-dice yellow bell pepper
¼ cup fine-dice red onion
¼ cup minced parsley
1 pound jumbo lump crabmeat, rinsed and picked
1 cup panko
Salt and black pepper, to taste
4 tablespoons salted butter or Herb Butter (page 27)
   (you may need more for a second batch)

Papaya-Mango Salsa (page 163)

Prepare crab cake

Preheat oven to 400°F.

In a large bowl, using a whisk, beat eggs, mayonnaise, mustard, Worcestershire and curry powder. Set aside and let curry bloom for 15 minutes.

Add scallions, peppers, red onion and parsley and toss. Add crab and panko and season to taste. Combine ingredients gently, so as to not break up the jumbo lump crab. Do this by hand; I wear kitchen gloves.

Form into eight 3-ounce patties. Do not overwork the mixture or it will break up. But do make sure you compress each patty firmly enough so that it stays together while searing.

In a hot skillet, melt butter until bubbling. Sear patties 4 at a time until golden brown, about 2 minutes, then flip and sear on other side until equally golden brown. Place directly into an ovenproof pan and place in the oven.

Finish cooking in the oven for about 8 minutes. Remove and plate immediately with the salsa placed on the top center of each crab cake. This is also nice served with a small frisée salad with fennel and arugula, tossed with a good olive oil, a squeeze of lime and a little sea salt, underneath or on the side.

Certified Angus Beef Tenderloin "Steak 'n' Eggs" Tartare

with Sunny-Side-Up Quail Egg

I know that some people are not as open to eating raw beef as they are to raw fish. The meat must be extremely high quality. Certified Angus Beef is always my go-to brand. Pairing it with a baked potato cup and fried egg also makes it easier for skeptics to be a bit more open—at least some elements are cooked! These truly yummy bites also work really well when served as canapés at a party.

SERVES FOUR

14 ounces prime grade Certified Angus Beef
   tenderloin fillet (can substitute choice grade CAB),
   very cold and diced small
1 tablespoon Worcestershire sauce
2 tablespoons fresh lemon juice
2 tablespoons Dijon mustard
1 tablespoon whole-grain Dijon mustard
¼ cup minced red onion
2 to 3 pinches cayenne pepper
3 tablespoons chopped capers
⅓ cup plus 3 tablespoons very good
   Spanish olive oil, divided
⅓ cup chopped parsley
Maldon salt, to taste
1½ dozen new potatoes (a little bigger than a golf
   ball; extra in case you break some)
Kosher salt and freshly ground black pepper, to taste
3 tablespoons salted butter

3 tablespoons water
1½ dozen quail eggs
   (this is more than you need to serve 4,
   but extra in case you break some yolks)
2 ounces micro arugula
2 handfuls curly frisée, torn apart
Lemon Dijon Vinaigrette (page 80)

Set up a small stainless-steel bowl that fits inside a slightly larger stainless-steel bowl that has some ice in it. Place beef in the small bowl. Mix Worcestershire, lemon juice, both mustards, red onion and capers into the cold beef. Mix well.

Drizzle in ⅓ cup olive oil, add parsley and season with Maldon. Mix lightly, then tightly cover the tartare bowl with plastic wrap. Store meat in refrigerator until ready to serve. This can be prepared up to 1½ hours before serving.

continued on page 64

continued from page 62

Preheat oven to 400°F and make sure your rack is in the middle. Use 1 tablespoon olive oil to coat a baking sheet.

Slice off a very small piece of the bottom of each potato so it stands level. Do the same for the tops so all the potatoes are about the same size, about that of a golf ball or smaller. Hollow them out by cupping potatoes firmly in the palm of your hand, then use a demitasse spoon or mellon baller to slowly scoop out the flesh. In the beginning, you are bound to break through and crack some, but practice makes perfect, so don't get frustrated—that's why you buy extra to start. When you hollow them, keep them all the same relative thickness. When you're done, place them in cold water so they don't discolor. When you have 12, that's enough, as you will serve 3 on each plate.

To cook the potatoes, take them out of the water and dry them a bit without cracking them. Then rub with 1 tablespoon olive oil and sprinkle with kosher salt and black pepper. Place potatoes upside down on the oiled baking sheet and transfer that to oven.

Cook for about 12 minutes or until fork-tender. When ready, remove from oven and allow to cool. When cool enough to handle, divide among 4 plates.

While potatoes are cooking, place a nonstick sauté pan over medium-high to high heat. Add butter and water. When hot, carefully place quail eggs in and sprinkle with some kosher salt and a few turns of black pepper. They will cook fairly quickly. When whites are cooked solid but yolks are still runny, remove pan from heat. Set aside.

In a bowl, quickly toss micro arugula with the remaining olive oil and season.

Remove tartare from refrigerator. Uncover and give it a mix. Taste again for flavor, adjusting if necessary.

Fill each potato cup to the rim with tartare mix. Top each with a quail egg and a small bundle of micro arugula. It's fine if the potato cups and quail eggs are warm. You just don't want them so hot that they cook the tartare. Toss frisée with some vinaigrette, then divide among plates. Serve immediately.

❋ This dish also pairs nicely with a hollowed-out Yukon Gold potato. Prepare and fill it the same way and top with a single chicken or duck egg.

SALADS

When it comes to salads, there are so many wonderful choices and combinations of fruits, vegetables, cheeses, meats, breads—endless ingredients, really—that are appropriate to include. The recipes I chose to share with you are salads I have created for my restaurants. Some have been staple menu items for years that regular customers crave and do not want removed, and others are specials. In my opinion, the first, most important tip to remember in creating a salad of your own is to go "seasonal." That way, your ingredients will be at their peak flavor, not force-ripened or picked way too early. You should also think about going "local" whenever possible, so that you will be supporting your produce farmers who are keeping America alive. With re-creating my recipes, you may not always be able to follow those mantras—especially if you need to acquire mangos and papayas during the dead of winter—but it's okay, I'll look the other way on those occasions!

Lemon-Roasted Garlic Caesar Salad

with Romaine Hearts, Fresh Squeezed Lemon, Roasted Garlic, Shaved Parmesan and Lemon Pepper-Sizzled Wontons

Crisp, cold Caesar salads are my thing. My dad always took us to this Italian restaurant in Berkeley Heights, New Jersey, called Linda's Fireside Inn. It was his favorite because the salads were always so nicely chilled and refreshing. To that end, I have always soaked my romaine in ice water first. Plus, the dressing has to be really lemony and the anchovies—well, I don't like canned anchovies at all, so when I can get those nice white ones in oil, that's when I make Caesar dressing. Serve it with roasted garlic on some toasted bread and there you have it: a dish for garlic lovers, and also to scare vampires away.

SERVES FOUR

Caesar Salad

1 recipe Lemon-Roasted Garlic
   Caesar Salad Dressing (page 81)
2 romaine hearts, core removed and cut in half
½ cup shaved Parmigiano-Reggiano
½ cup Lemon Pepper-Sizzled Wontons
4 heads roasted garlic (see below)
4 small baguettes, toasted

Lemon Pepper-Sizzled Wontons

1 pack wonton skins
Vegetable oil, for frying
McCormick's Lemon & Pepper seasoning

continued on page 70

How to Roast Garlic

Preheat oven to 400°F. Remove outer papery layers of skin from garlic head. Keep cloves intact. Cut off top quarter of garlic head. Rub head with olive oil. Sprinkle the exposed garlic top with kosher or sea salt and cover with foil. (If you have a muffin tin, use that for extra-easy preparation, as the heads will stay upright.) Roast in the oven for 30 to 35 minutes.

continued from page 68

Prepare Caesar salad

Prepare a bowl of ice water. Soak romaine hearts in the ice water while preparing the dressing. Then remove hearts, hold by the stems and shake hard, expelling water. Pat dry with a clean towel.

Prepare wontons

Cut wontons into ¼-inch strips. In a deep skillet, heat enough oil to fry strips. Once oil reaches frying temperature, cook in batches until golden brown. Remove from oil with a slotted spoon, place on paper towels to drain and sprinkle with seasoning while still hot.

Assemble

Prepare 4 salad plates with 1 romaine heart per plate, either hand-torn or with leaves still intact, per your preference. Drizzle each heart with dressing, then garnish with Parmigiano-Reggiano and wontons. Place 1 roasted garlic head and 1 baguette on each plate and serve.

Learn the secrets behind
Chef Cindy Hutson's
Cuisine of the Sun

Future Class TBD
Classes begin at 11:30 am until approximately 2:30 pm

Ortanique Interactive Cooking Class

Saturday, June 14th, 2014

"MEXICAN IRON CHEF OFF WITH GUEST JUDGES CINDY AND DELIUS"
MEET and GREET
11:30am

Menu:

MEXICAN TORTILLA SOUP
With Crunchy Corn Tortilla Strips, Lime and Cilantro

PAN SEARED SALAD GREENS
De Queso Blanco and Scallion Harissa Dressing

PINEAPPLE MARINATED Adobo Grilled

Farm-Fresh Egg and Crispy Duck Confit, Haricots Verts and "Bubble 'n' Squeak" Salad

Tossed in Lemon-Dijon Vinaigrette

It is classically Continental to have a coddled, fried or poached egg on a salad. (When I'm traveling in Europe, I make it my mission to eat plenty of them!) One year, back in my homeland, Miami restaurants were celebrating "BritWeek" and I needed to come up with a three-course menu. This dish was inspired both by those salads and by my last trip to England, where I had "bubble 'n' squeak" (fried leftover winter vegetables, usually those lingering from a midday Sunday roast) topped with a coddled egg. It was so delicious, I decided to re-create it as a green entrée and add some additional appeal with duck confit.

SERVES FOUR

Duck Confit

6–8 whole duck legs, thigh and leg attached,
   5–7 pounds all together
2 teaspoons black peppercorns
1 tablespoon allspice berries
4 bay leaves, crumbled
⅔ cup sea salt
1 large head garlic, broken apart,
   cloves smashed with flat side of knife
   (peel excess skin but it's not necessary to remove all)
1 bunch fresh thyme
Peel of 1 orange, no pith
Peel of 1 lemon, no pith
¼ cup brandy (optional)

1 (10-pound) pail rendered duck fat
   (can be purchased online)
A couple handfuls dry white navy beans,
   enough to create a barrier between
   the cooked duck and a container bottom

Haricots Verts and Bubble 'n' Squeak Salad

3 tablespoons duck fat, plus extra for sautéing
¾ cup small-dice onion
2 cloves fresh garlic, minced
1 cup duck confit, picked from bones, bones discarded
½ cup frozen peas, defrosted

continued on page 74

continued from page 72

8–10 Brussels sprouts,
   cooked and quartered or sliced

2 tablespoons fresh thyme leaves

¾ cup leftover mashed potatoes

1 cup new potatoes,
   boiled in salted water and cooled

Kosher salt and freshly ground black pepper, to taste

½–1 cup Lemon-Dijon Vinaigrette (page 80)

1 (8-ounce) pack haricots verts,
   cooked al dente in salted water

4 handfuls frisée

4 large eggs, cooked sunny side up
   (or to your preference)

Prepare duck confit

Rinse duck legs and pat dry with paper towels.

In a spice grinder, pulse peppercorns, allspice, bay leaves and about 5 tablespoons salt until crumbled together, but not ground fine. Rub mix onto all duck legs.

On the bottom of a glass or stainless-steel baking dish large enough to hold all the duck legs, spread half of the remaining salt. Top with half the garlic, half the thyme and half the citrus peels.

Press duck legs, skin sides down and in a single layer, into seasoned dish. If using the brandy, drizzle it now across the duck. Cover duck with remaining salt, garlic, thyme and citrus peels. Again, press this into the legs. Cover with plastic wrap and cure in refrigerator for 48 hours.

When ready to cook, make sure oven rack is in the center. Preheat oven to 300°F. Remove duck from refrigerator and rinse off the salt and seasonings. Pat dry thoroughly.

Place an 8-quart Dutch oven large enough to fit the duck legs over a medium flame on the stovetop. Fill half the dish with duck fat. Sink legs in, skin side down. They do not have to be in a single layer now, but they must be covered with the melted fat. Once fat begins to bubble in the slightest, transfer the duck legs into the oven, covered, and cook for 3½ to 4 hours, until fat and meat begin to creep up the bone.

Once cooked, let cool at room temperature until you are able to handle the legs. Remove from fat and place on a wire rack.

Place some dry beans in the bottom of a clean container large enough to store your duck legs and fat. These will keep the duck from actually touching the container's bottom, allowing some of the duck fat to solidify between the bottom of the container and the legs, preserving the legs and keeping them safe from any bacteria growing. Place duck legs on top of beans. Through a strainer lined with cheesecloth, pour liquid duck fat into container over legs and place in refrigerator, uncovered, until the fat solidifies. Then cover and store until needed.

Makes 6 to 8 duck legs

Prepare haricots verts and bubble 'n' squeak salad

Preheat oven to 400°F.

In a large skillet over medium heat, melt 1 tablespoon duck fat and sauté onions and garlic until tender. Remove from heat and turn into a bowl. Add duck confit, peas, Brussels sprouts, thyme and mashed potatoes. Mix gently together.

With a fork, coarsely mash new potatoes into bowl, mixing them into the other ingredients. Sprinkle with a little salt, if needed, and a few turns of the peppermill. Using a ring mold, shape mixture into the size of a 1½-inch-thick hockey puck. Compress gently. Remove ring mold and repeat 3 times for a total of 4 bubble 'n' squeaks.

Using the same skillet, melt 2 tablespoons remaining duck fat and pan-sear each bubble 'n' squeak on both sides. Place in oven to heat throughout.

Meanwhile, prepare vinaigrette. Toss frisée and haricots verts with desired amount of dressing. Divide among 4 plates.

Prepare eggs to your preference.

Remove cooked bubble 'n' squeaks from oven and slide on top of each salad. Finish with cooked egg. For an extra touch, add a little sautéed duck confit to the plate.

* Since it is such a long, albeit easy, process to cook duck confit, I usually make extra to enjoy in other ways, or in the same way a few weeks later. The confit and fat together will keep in the refrigerator for about a month. Any extra fat from the gallon bucket is awesome used in place of butter or oil—for cooking french fries, chicken, oven-roasted potatoes, you name it!

Marinated Quinoa Salad

with Goldbar Squash, Zucchini, Pine Nuts,
Ricotta Salata and Agrumato Oil Microgreens

I sometimes have to remind myself about quinoa. One of the few crops that survive the high altitudes of the Andes mountains, it was enjoyed by the Incas for thousands of years before it was discovered by trendy foodies. It's not actually a grain, as some people think, but a seed. In fact, it's higher in protein than most grains and is usually grown organically. It's also naturally free of gluten and cholesterol, and possesses all nine amino acids. It sounds almost perfect, right? Well, I think this salad is too, but nonvegetarians should feel free to add animal proteins to make it a heartier dish.

SERVES FOUR

4 cups Anson Mills quinoa
  (or other high-quality),
  cooked as directed on the package
1 pound zucchini, cut into thumbnail-size cubes,
  soft seed center removed
1 pound Goldbar squash, cut into matchsticks,
  soft seed center removed
2 tablespoons kosher salt, divided
Juice of ½ lemon, plus 4 tablespoons
  freshly squeezed lemon juice, divided
4 handfuls microgreens and herbs,
  your choice, including micro arugula,
  Bull's Blood and cilantro

1 tablespoon Agrumato oil
⅓ cup toasted pine nuts
1 cup chopped Italian parsley leaves, divided
¼ cup chopped fresh basil
8 ounces ricotta salata, cut into small cubes
6 tablespoons freshly grated Parmesan
1 cup diced tomatoes
1 tablespoon finely grated lemon zest
1 teaspoon sherry vinegar
1 teaspoon white sugar
Salt and pepper, to taste
⅓ cup extra virgin olive oil

continued on page 78

continued from page 76

Spread quinoa on a baking sheet to cool. Set aside.

In a stainless-steel bowl, place zucchini and squash and toss with 1 tablespoon kosher salt and juice of ½ lemon. Set aside for 8 to 10 minutes.

Rinse zucchini and squash in ice-cold water and pat dry with paper towels. In a large bowl, place zucchini and squash with pine nuts, parsley, basil, ricotta salata, Parmesan and tomatoes. Toss.

In another bowl, whisk zest, remaining lemon juice, sherry vinegar, sugar, remaining salt, and pepper to taste. Slowly drizzle olive oil into lemon juice mixture while whisking. Pour over zucchini mixture and toss.

Transfer quinoa to a bowl. Add quinoa to vegetable mixture and toss well.

Remove microgreens from refrigerator. Toss microgreens with 1 tablespoon Agrumato oil and salt to taste. Divide vegetable quinoa salad among individual plates or 1 nice platter. Top with shaved Parmesan and seasoned microgreens.

Vinaigrettes and Dressings

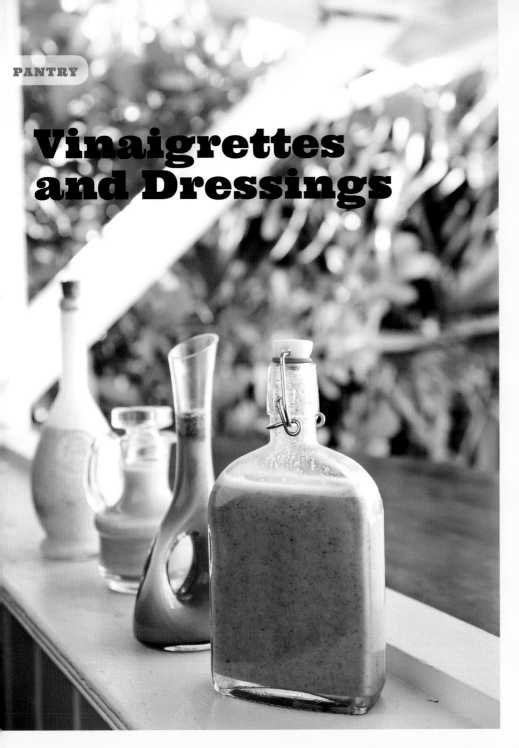

Balsamic Vinaigrette

¼ cup roasted garlic (page 68)

2 whole roasted shallots (page 68)

Salt and pepper, to taste

12 large basil leaves

½ cup balsamic vinegar

¼ cup water

1 teaspoon tomato paste

¼ cup sugar

1¼ cups garlic oil (page 80)

In a blender, pulverize garlic, shallots, salt, pepper and basil. Add vinegar, water, tomato paste and sugar, and purée. Then slowly drizzle in infused oil and blend. Taste and adjust pepper if necessary.

   Makes 3 cups

❋ Use with the Crispy Calamari (page 90) or a recipe of your choice.

Worcestershire Vinaigrette

2 roasted shallots (page 68)

3 cloves roasted garlic
   (page 68)

1 tablespoon Colman's
   dry mustard powder

1 teaspoon kosher salt

¼ cup Worcestershire sauce

1 ounce beef demi-glace
   (store-bought is fine; see note)

½ cup white balsamic vinegar

1 teaspoon sugar

Freshly ground black pepper, to taste

¾ cup canola-olive oil blend

Mince shallot and garlic and place in a stainless-steel bowl. Add mustard and salt and mix into a paste. Incorporate Worcestershire, demi-glace, balsamic vinegar, sugar and pepper.

   Whisking slowly, add oil until vinaigrette is emulsified. Place in refrig-

I collect mortar and pestle sets. When I travel, that and salts are what I look for to bring back home with me. Some salad dressings, such as the Lemon-Dijon Vinaigrette, I enjoy preparing with a mortar and pestle. In fact, I have a rather large one I bought in a market in Jamaica made out of lignum vitae wood that I have designated for this dressing alone. For other dressings, I may hand-whisk them, or use a blender or a food processor for convenience. It depends on the individual dressing, and what the thickening agent is—eggs, oil, yogurt or something else.

continued on page 80

continued from page 79

erator until ready to use.

Makes about 1½ cups

✳ For store-bought stock or demi-glace, only one brand will do for me: Demi-Glace Gold. It's a four-strength reduction, so you can use it as a classic veal demi-glace or dilute it to make stock. Use with the Ortanique Certified Angus Beef Steak Salad (page 86) or a recipe of your choice.

Orange-Ginger Vinaigrette

¼ cup chopped roasted garlic
   (page 68)
1 roasted shallot, chopped
   (page 68)
1 teaspoon freshly grated ginger
1 teaspoon onion powder
1 teaspoon garlic powder
1 teaspoon ground ginger powder
½ cup freshly squeezed orange juice
½ cup orange marmalade
1 tablespoon kosher salt
½ tablespoon ground,
   toasted coriander
¼ cup honey
1 tablespoon sugar
¾ cup apple cider vinegar
1¾ cups canola-vegetable oil blend

In a blender, place all ingredients except oil and blend on low speed until mixed. While blender is running, slowly

drizzle in oil until fully incorporated.

Makes 1 quart

✳ Use with the Braised Octopus Tiradito (page 45) or a recipe of your choice.

Lemon-Dijon Vinaigrette

1 clove fresh garlic, or more to taste
¾ teaspoon Maldon salt
1 large hardboiled egg yolk
1½ teaspoon Dijon mustard
   (I prefer Grey Poupon)
1 teaspoon sugar
6 tablespoons freshly squeezed
   lemon juice
Freshly ground black pepper, to taste
8 tablespoons extra virgin olive oil

With a mortar and pestle, grind garlic clove and salt to make a paste. Add egg yolk and mustard and continue mashing. Add sugar and mash until you no longer feel the sugar granules.

Add lemon juice and a few turns of the peppermill. At this point, if you have a whisk that will fit in the bowl of the mortar, you should switch to that. Whisk while drizzling in olive oil slowly until it has incorporated.

Makes 1 cup

✳ Use with the Farm Fresh Egg and Crispy Duck Confit, Haricots Verts and "Bubble 'n' Squeak" Salad (page 72) or a recipe of your choice.

Lavender-Honey Vinaigrette

¾ cup champagne vinegar
2 tablespoons dried lavender flowers
1 tablespoon kosher salt
¼ teaspoon freshly ground black pepper
1 cup honey
1 cup walnut oil

In a food processor, pulverize vinegar, lavender, salt and pepper for about 2 minutes. Strain through a chinoise and add strained liquid back to bowl of processor.

Add honey and mix for 1 minute. Drizzle in oil while motor is running until incorporated.

Store in a plastic container with a tight-fitting lid in the refrigerator.

Makes 2¾ cups.

✳ Use with the Oven-Baked Brie Salad (page 88) or a recipe of your choice.

Minted Passion Fruit Vinaigrette

¼ cup roasted garlic (page 68)
¼ cup loosely packed roasted shallots
   (page 68)
½ cup loosely packed, picked
   mint leaves
¼ cup sugar
1½ tablespoons kosher salt
¼ teaspoon freshly ground
   black pepper

How to Make Shallot and/or Garlic Oil

In a small saucepan, place desired amount of shallot and/or garlic with your choice of variety and quantity of oil. I like to use a half-and-half mixture of canola and olive oils that I call "blended oil." Bring to a boil, then immediately lower heat to a simmer. Stir until cloves are soft. Remove from heat and bring down to room temperature. When cool, strain garlic or shallot and reserve for use in recipes; reserve oil for same.

½ cup passion fruit purée
½ cup rice vinegar
¼ cup cold water
¼ cup mirin
½ cup walnut oil
1½ cups canola-olive oil blend

In a blender, place garlic, shallots, mint, sugar, salt, pepper and passion fruit purée. Blend until pulverized.

With motor running, drizzle in vinegar, water and mirin and blend until well mixed. Drizzle in walnut and blended oils and mix until incorporated.

Store in a plastic container with a tight-fitting lid in the refrigerator.

Makes 3 cups

✱ Use with the Norma's Terrace Salad (page 82) or a recipe of your choice.

Lemon-Roasted Garlic Caesar Salad Dressing

2 large roasted garlic cloves
    (page 68)
1 small fresh garlic clove
1 flat tablespoon kosher salt
1 fresh white anchovy fillet
    packed in oil
    (found in gourmet markets or online)
4 tablespoons freshly squeezed
    lemon juice
2 large egg yolks
1 tablespoon Worcestershire sauce
4 tablespoons cold water
2 tablespoons Dijon mustard

¼ cup vegetable oil
½ cup olive oil
½ cup grated Parmigiano-Reggiano

In a Vitamix or food processor, mix roasted and fresh garlics with salt, anchovy, lemon juice, egg yolks, Worcestershire, water and Dijon on medium speed. Once smooth, slowly begin drizzling in the oils in a steady stream until emulsified.

Using a spatula, scrape into a small bowl and whisk in grated cheese. Refrigerate in an airtight container until ready to use. The dressing keeps for about 2 weeks.

Makes 2 cups

✱ Use with the Lemon Roasted Garlic Caesar Salad (page 68) or a recipe of your choice.

Pomegranate Greek Yogurt Dressing

8 roasted garlic cloves, sliced in half
    (page 68)
¾ cup halved roasted shallots
    (page 68)
¼ cup prepared Dijon mustard
½ cup orange marmalade
½ cup pomegranate juice
¾ cup honey
3 tablespoons kosher salt
½ teaspoon freshly ground
    black pepper

1 container fat-free pomegranate
    Greek yogurt
    (high quality; I prefer the brand Fage)
¼ cup sugar
¾ cup apple cider vinegar
1¾ cups strained, blended
    shallot-garlic oil (page 80)

In a Vitamix or blender on low speed, combine all ingredients except the oil. Once the ingredients are smoothly puréed, slowly drizzle in oil until fully incorporated and thickened.

Makes 3 cups

✱ Use with the Vanilla Bean-Marinated Grilled Pineapple Salad (page 95) or a recipe of your choice.

Homemade Russian Dressing

1 cup Basic Aioli (page 108)
2 tablespoons brunoised yellow onion
¼ cup ketchup
1 teaspoon Scotch bonnet
    hot sauce (store-bought is fine)
2 teaspoons ground horseradish
½ teaspoon smoked paprika
1 tablespoon Worcestershire sauce
1 tablespoon kosher salt

In a bowl, combine all ingredients.

Makes 1¼ cups

✱ Use with the "Jersey Style" Triple Decker Sloppy Joe (page 98) or a recipe of your choice.

Norma's Terrace Salad

of Local Greens, Endive, Candied Pecans, Shaved Fennel,
Papaya, Mango and Cucumber Curls

This salad is named after Norma Shirley, mother of my partner and love, Delius Shirley. Norma was dubbed "Julia Child of the Caribbean"—and rightfully so. She brought Caribbean cooking to another level with her creativity, passion, representation and presentation of her beloved Jamaica. This salad was inspired by Norma. I cannot do her version justice, but I will try in its translation. The Norma Shirley Fund was set up in her honor. Delius donates $1 for each salad sold in our establishments to the fund, which benefits culinary students' school fees at the University of Technology in Kingston, Jamaica.

SERVES FOUR

2 endive bulbs, roots cut off, julienned
2 cups mixed local baby greens
1 cup local arugula (baby arugula is milder)
Kosher salt and freshly ground black pepper, to taste
1 cup sweet fresh grapefruit, cut into segments
½ cup crumbled feta cheese
   (do not buy pre-crumbled)
1 cup Minted Passion Fruit Vinaigrette (page 80)
1 firm, ripe solo papaya, peeled, seeded
   and cut into wedges
1 firm, ripe seasonal mango, peeled, seeded
   and cut into wedges
1 firm, ripe avocado, peeled, seeded
   and cut into wedges
1 cup European cucumber curls (if you have a
   Chinese vertical cutter, it's a fun kitchen tool)
1 cup red or gold beet curls (same as above)
1 cup Caribbean Candied Pecans (page 84)

In a stainless-steel bowl, mix endive, baby greens and arugula. Sprinkle with a little salt and a few turns of the pepper mill, seasoning to taste. Then toss with grapefruit, feta and ½ cup salad dressing.

On the inside border of 4 plates, alternate papaya, mango and avocado wedges, dividing fruits evenly among the plates. Drizzle with ¼ cup dressing. Place mixed greens in center of each plate, piling them high.

Toss cucumber curls with 2 tablespoons dressing and arrange like a flower on top. Do the same with beet curls and remaining dressing. Garnish with spiced nuts.

✳ Don't cut endive in advance or it will brown. It has to be done right before the salad is put together.

✳ This salad pairs very well with the Jamaican Jerk Paste-Marinated and Seared Bluefin Tuna (page 140) or the West Indian Curried Crab Cake (page 60), both of which are also garnished with papaya and mango.

Caribbean Candied Pecans

I make these using a 2-pound bag of pecans; because people love them so much, I always wind up giving them some to take home. I put them in pretty flip-top jars and label them for gifts. They are also a delicious way to top sweet potatoes during the holidays.

2 pounds raw pecans
1 tablespoon cinnamon
1 tablespoon ground ginger
1 tablespoon Old Bay Seasoning
1 tablespoon ground cloves
1 teaspoon ground coriander
1 teaspoon ground allspice
1 cup Jamaican brown sugar
⅓ cup simple syrup
   (supersaturated, boiled sugar water)

In a 325°F oven, toast pecans until aromatic, 6 to 8 minutes.

Meanwhile, combine all dry ingredients in a bowl.

When pecans are toasted, remove from oven but do not turn off the heat.

Moisten pecans with simple syrup, then coat them with the spice-sugar mixture. Return to oven and bake for another 6 to 8 minutes.

When done, cool completely before sealing in an airtight container. If they are not completely cool when sealed, they will create steam and become soggy.

Ortanique Certified Angus Beef Steak Salad

with Pommes Frites, Red Onions, Romaine Hearts, Crumbled Blue Cheese and Worcestershire Vinaigrette

When I dream up recipes, I try to think about combinations of foods that I grew up with and/or that complement each other. So here is a salad that could also work as a summer dinner or a substantial lunch. I use this wonderfully marbled flank steak, grilled or pan-seared, then complete it with crisp, chilled romaine hearts, crumbled blue cheese, grilled red onion and a vinaigrette that I make with a base of Worcestershire sauce and demi-glace that I usually have frozen in an ice cube tray. I fry up some crispy pommes frites to serve with it, and I believe it's even better than a classic steak-and-salad combo on a menu in a great chophouse.

SERVES FOUR

1 (16-ounce) flank steak
Salt and pepper, to taste
3 tablespoons canola oil, for frying
1 large red onion, sliced into ¼-inch-thick rings
2 large vine-ripe tomatoes, cut into 12 wedges
4 ounces imported blue cheese, crumbled
2 heads romaine hearts, rinsed and dried
Worcestershire Vinaigrette (page 79), to taste
1 bag store-bought shoestring potatoes, prepared
   as pommes frites according to directions
1 recipe Chipotle Aioli (page 109)

Prepare a grill or oven for cooking the meat. Season steak on both sides with salt and pepper. Cook to de-sired temperature. Remove from heat and let rest for 5 minutes. Slice on a bias and divide into 4 portions.

In a skillet, heat canola oil over high. Sear both sides of onion rings as a unit, without allowing them to fall apart. Set aside.

Tear romaine hearts by hand and place in a large stainless-steel bowl. Add half blue cheese and season. Drizzle in vinaigrette and toss to evenly coat.

Divide salad among 4 plates and top with remaining blue cheese and tomato wedges. Top that with grilled onion and fan out steak along base of salad. Place handful pommes frites on back side of plate. Drizzle more vinaigrette on top, if desired. Serve with chipotle aioli for dipping pommes frittes.

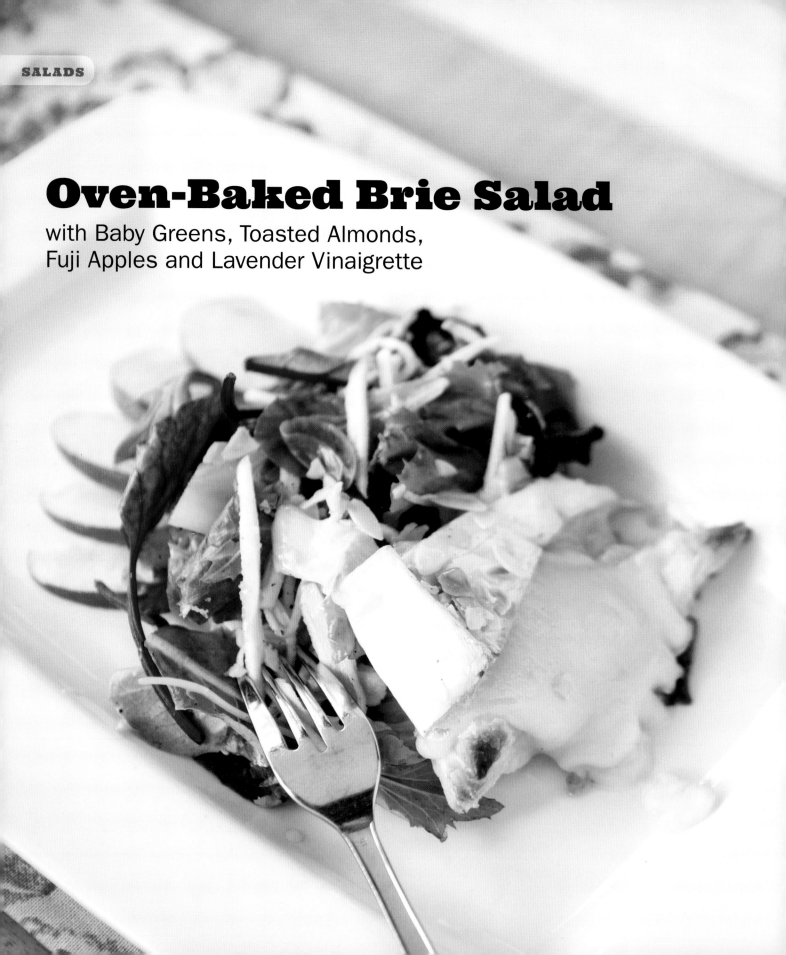

Oven-Baked Brie Salad

with Baby Greens, Toasted Almonds,
Fuji Apples and Lavender Vinaigrette

Everyone loves warm, melted Brie in puff pastry. Many cooks like to serve it completely wrapped up in those flaky layers of dough, but I prefer it with less pastry and more immediately available melting, gooey cheese. Topping the cheese with toasted almonds and crisp apples, some earthy greens and the lavender vinaigrette makes this a charming and agreeable brunch salad. Pair it with a great Sauvignon Blanc or Viognier for even more enchantment.

SERVES FOUR

1 recipe Lavender-Honey Vinaigrette (page 80)
2 puff pastry sheets (frozen, store-bought)
1 (9-inch) wheel French Brie cheese
2 Fuji apples (substitute crisp apple of your choice, or pear)
1 large lemon
4 handfuls mixed baby field greens
8 ounces toasted slivered almonds

Prepare vinaigrette. While doing so, allow puff pastry to thaw slightly.

Preheat oven to 400°F.

Cut Brie into 4 equal pieces. Place a piece of cheese on top of semifrozen puff pastry. Cut puff pastry into a triangle shape, slightly larger than the cheese. Repeat on remaining pastry for each cheese wedge. Remove cheese and set aside. Using a fork, dock puff pastry (poke holes in the dough) all around.

Place pastry triangles on a baking sheet and par-bake until a very light golden brown, about 5 minutes. Remove from oven and set aside, but don't turn off the oven.

Julienne apples and squeeze a little lemon juice on them so they don't discolor.

In a salad bowl, place greens. Add almonds and apples.

Place reserved cheese on puff pastry. Return pastry triangles to the oven and bake until cheese begins to melt, pastry begins to rise around edges of cheese, and triangles turn a nice golden brown. Remove from oven.

Toss greens with dressing and divide among 4 salad plates. Make sure some nuts and apples that have settled at the bottom of the bowl are on top of each of the salads. Place one Brie cheese puff pastry on each of the salads and serve immediately.

✳ For frozen puff pastry, Pepperidge Farm is always dependable.

Crispy Calamari Dusted in Caribbean Spices
with Mixed Greens and Balsamic Vinaigrette

Everyone seems to like a plate of lightly crisped calamari. Even most children, funny enough, do as well. This preparation may not be best suited for kids given the jerk seasoning, however, as it does have a little kick. Still, it's balanced out with the addition of the balsamic vinaigrette–dressed salad placed on top. If you just can't get away from the traditional marinara and lemon that frequently accompany fried calamari, by all means make the calamari and omit the salad. I think you should try the whole recipe at least once, though—the combo is great.

SERVES FOUR TO SIX

Spiced Crispy Calamari
4 pounds calamari tubes
   and/or tentacles, cleaned and beaks removed
2 cups all-purpose flour
1 cup garbanzo bean flour
1 cup panko
½ teaspoon paprika
½ teaspoon smoked paprika
½ teaspoon garlic powder
½ teaspoon onion powder
1 rounded tablespoon jerk seasoning powder
1 teaspoon Old Bay Seasoning
1 rounded tablespoon baking powder
2 tablespoons kosher salt
Peanut or vegetable oil
   (enough to fill a FryDaddy or other electric fryer)

Mixed Greens
1 clamshell container mixed baby lettuce
2 heads romaine hearts, washed, dried and chopped
1 pint mixed heirloom cherry tomatoes, sliced in half
   (or your favorite small tomatoes)
1 package baby Kirby cucumbers,
   washed, skin on, sliced thin
   (can be found at gourmet markets or Whole Foods)
3–6 radishes, sliced thin on a mandoline (optional)
½–¾ cup Balsamic Vinaigrette (page 79)

continued on page 92

continued from page 90

Prepare spiced crispy calamari

Cut squid tubes horizontally about ½ inch in width, no wider. If you also buy tentacles, make sure beak has been removed by feeling in the center for a plastic-feeling piece (it really does look like a beak). Also, there is a very long, central tentacle; cut that out and discard. After squid is cut, place in a bowl and set in refrigerator.

Preheat oven to 250°F.

In a 9-by-13-inch pan, combine flours, panko, spices, jerk and Old Bay seasonings, baking powder, and salt. Dredge calamari, tossing and coating well. Place floured calamari in a strainer basket and shake gently to remove any clumping flour. Separate it into 2 to 3 batches for frying so as not to overcrowd the fryer.

Heat oil in your FryDaddy to 325°F. Line a tray with paper towels.

In batches, fry calamari until a crisp golden brown. Place on paper towels to drain, then transfer to another baking sheet and place in oven while you fry consecutive batches until complete.

Divide cooked calamari among 4 plates and top with the dressed salad.

✳ Another simple way to enjoy this calamari is to make one of the aioli recipes in this book (see pages 108–09) and use as a dipping sauce. The Roasted Garlic and Scotch Bonnet Aioli tops them all if you are a spice lover!

Prepare mixed greens

In a bowl, mix greens, tomatoes, cucumbers and radish together. Toss with desired amount of dressing. Set aside until ready to serve.

Vanilla Bean-Marinated Grilled Pineapple Salad

with Bruised Kale, Arugula, Heirloom Tomatoes and Cypress Grove Muesli Croutons in Pomegranate Greek Yogurt Dressing

During pineapple season at The Dunmore hotel on Harbour Island, when our produce order comes into the kitchen, all you can smell are those gorgeous, sweet Eleutheran pineapples. The island also grows some of the best arugula I have had anywhere, spicy as can be, so the combination of the two, it occurred to me, would be simply terrific. I found some pomegranate Fage yogurt in the walk-in refrigerator and knew instantly that it would be the right addition for dressing this salad, which is so refreshing on a hot summer's day.

SERVES FOUR

8 (½-inch) slices fresh pineapple
1 vanilla bean, insides scraped out and reserved
3 tablespoons white sugar
4 slices muesli bread, cut into 1-inch cubes
4 tablespoons extra-virgin olive oil, divided
1 bag kale, washed and dried
1–2 teaspoons kosher salt
4 handfuls mixed baby greens, washed and dried
4 handfuls baby arugula, washed and dried
2½ cups chunked heirloom tomatoes
¾–1 cup Pomegranate Greek Yogurt Dressing
   (page 81)
8 ounces Cypress Grove's Midnight Moon goat cheese,
   cut into 1-inch-thick slices
   (to fit on top of each crouton)
½ cup pomegranate seeds

Preheat oven to 300°F.

In a bowl, toss pineapple slices with sugar and scraped vanilla bean. Set aside.

In another bowl, toss bread cubes with 2 tablespoons olive oil, then place on a baking sheet and toast in the oven until a light golden brown. Remove croutons when done and set aside.

Place a grill fry pan over high heat and, once extremely hot, brush pan with 1 tablespoon olive oil. Add pineapple slices and char on both sides. Remove and cut into cubes, then set aside.

To prepare kale for raw eating, remove the thick center core by tearing off the leaves. Then put remaining olive oil in the palm of your hands with a little salt. Take kale leaves in your hands a few at a time and rub your hands and the kale back and forth. This tenderizes the kale and makes it turn bright green. Place kale, mixed baby greens and arugula in a bowl and toss with tomatoes and dressing. Divide among 4 salad plates and top with grilled pineapple.

Place cheese on croutons and heat just until cheese melts. Divide cheese croutons among salad plates. Finish by garnishing with pomegranate seeds, then serve.

CHAPTER 4

I have always loved a great sandwich. Growing up in New Jersey, I had unlimited access to great Italian and Jewish delis and bakeries. Early in the morning, the aromas would waft through the air, and the breads would still be so warm from the oven that they couldn't be sliced yet. That's when bread became a canvas for me to slather on some really great aiolis, mustards, melted cheeses, meats, fruits and veggies. Today, I believe there's no end to what one, two or even three layers of the soft, crunchy, grainy, nutty, yeasty slices of heaven that we call bread can contain. All you need is imagination. Here are some of my favorites.

ICHES
NINI

"Jersey Style" Triple Decker Sloppy Joe

with Roasted Turkey, Braised Beef Tongue, Coleslaw, Homemade Russian Dressing and Rye Bread

My dad used to own a men's haberdashery in Summit, New Jersey. Around the corner was a place called Hill City Delicatessen. They had the best sandwiches. My dad would bring home these parchment-wrapped, triple-decker wonders after work on Saturday for us to eat on Sunday while we were watching football. They were cut into quarters, and better the second day than the first because all the flavors had melded together. As kids, we would ask, "What's the pink meat?" He would just say, "It's meat," and we wouldn't question it any further. Years later, after high school, I found out that it was tongue. It was so good back then, and I still enjoy it to this day, but I always did wonder what those taste bud–looking things were.

MAKES TWO SANDWICHES

Braised Beef Tongue

1 (3–4 pound) beef tongue

¼ cup vegetable oil

2 large yellow onions, quartered, skin on

8 cloves garlic, smashed with flat side of knife

4 stalks celery, with leaves, coarsely chopped

3 carrots, peeled and coarsely chopped

3 bay leaves

1 bunch fresh thyme

10 black peppercorns

8 cloves garlic

4–6 quarts beef stock, fresh or store-bought

❋ I know some may feel that cooking an actual tongue of any animal in a braiser is a bit much. I say, if we are going to process an animal for consumption, pay homage to that animal and utilize it to its fullest. So here is a recipe should you choose to make your own beef tongue. If you can't bring yourself to do it or can't find it, feel free to substitute corned beef or pastrami.

Homemade Russian Dressing

1 cup Basic Aioli (page 108)

2 tablespoons brunoised yellow onion

¼ cup ketchup

1 teaspoon Scotch bonnet hot sauce
   (store-bought is fine)

2 teaspoons horseradish

½ teaspoon smoked paprika

1 tablespoon Worcestershire sauce

1 tablespoon kosher salt

"Jersey Style" Triple Decker Sloppy Joe

6 slices fresh-baked Jewish rye bread

4 tablespoons Homemade Russian Dressing

4 thin slices Swiss cheese

4 thin slices roasted turkey breast

1 pint of your favorite coleslaw

4 thin slices Braised Beef Tongue
   (can substitute corned beef or pastrami—or both!)

continued on page 100

continued from page 99

Prepare homemade Russian dressing

In a bowl, combine all ingredients.

Makes 1¼ cups

Prepare braised beef tongue

Place tongue in a clean sink and scrub thoroughly with a clean nail brush.

Transfer tongue to a pot and cover with cold water. Bring to a boil. Remove tongue from water and set aside.

Meanwhile, heat oil in a 10-quart pot with a lid. Sauté onion, garlic, celery and carrots until tender. Add herbs and the tongue, then cover with stock. Bring to a boil and cover, then lower to a simmer. Cook for 1 hour per pound or until tender.

Once cooked, remove and plunge into ice water. When cool enough to handle, use a sharp knife to slice away the connective tissue underneath. Then slice tongue as thin as possible for your sandwich.

Makes 6 to 8 servings

Strain broth and save for soup stock; it makes for an excellent beef soup. As far as the connective tissue goes, save that, too—it's a wonderful treat for your dog if you have one.

Prepare Sloppy Joe

Place 1 slice bread on a plate and smear with 1 tablespoon dressing. Place 2 slices cheese on top. Then place 2 slices turkey and about 2 ounces coleslaw.

Place a second piece of rye bread on top of the coleslaw. Smear with another tablespoon dressing, then add 2 slices beef tongue. On top of tongue place 1 ounce coleslaw and close sandwich with a third piece of bread.

Repeat process for the second sandwich. Cut both sandwiches into triangular halves and serve.

50/50 Bombay Burgers

with Toasted Curry-Spiced Certified Angus Beef Chuck and
Niman Ranch Ground Lamb Topped with Mango-Cherry-Chili Chutney
and Goat Cheese-Chipotle Aioli

This burger came to me when I was asked to participate in the South Beach Wine &
Food Festival's very popular Burger Bash a few years ago. I wanted to do something
different, something eclectic, some "Cuisine of the Sun." So I called Certified Angus Beef
and got them to blend some meat for me. Then I toasted off some curry seasonings,
added some ground lamb and got my crew together. We sat in the back of a refrigerator
truck and made 3,500 burgers for the event. They were so good, my regular customers
who tasted them there asked me to put them on the menu. Of course, we did.

SERVES FOUR

50/50 Bombay Burgers

4 tablespoons salted butter

¾ brunoised sweet onion

1 large clove garlic, minced

½ cup brunoised celery

½ cup brunoised carrot

1 pound Certified Angus beef (80 percent lean)

1 pound Niman Ranch ground lamb

½ cup chopped cilantro

1 serrano chili, seeded and minced

1 teaspoon smoked paprika

1 teaspoon Madras curry powder

½ teaspoon ground cumin

1 teaspoon toasted and ground coriander

1½ tablespoons salt

1 recipe Goat Cheese-Chipotle Aioli
   (page 109)

Mango-Cherry-Chili Chutney

4 tablespoons Herb Butter (page 27)

2 cups diced red onion

½ cup thin-sliced garlic

4 cups medium-diced mango

2 chipotle chili peppers in adobo sauce, chopped
   (sauce will stick to peppers)

¼ cup tomato paste

continued on page 104

continued from page 102
1½ cups white wine

⅓ cup apple cider vinegar

2 cups minced Amarena cherries

2 tablespoons coriander, ground

2 tablespoons curry powder

2 tablespoons kosher salt

1 bunch cilantro, chopped

✻ You can buy good-quality canned chipotle peppers in adobo sauce in your local market. Look in the Spanish foods section or in the beans and canned vegetable section. Goya is a favored brand but there are several others that make a decent product. You can also cook up your own chipotle in adobo by searching for recipes on the Internet.

Prepare 50/50 Bombay burgers

In a skillet, melt butter and sauté onions, garlic and celery until soft. Add carrots and sauté until soft. Remove from heat, transfer to a plate and place in the refrigerator to cool.

In a large bowl, place the two meats. Add cilantro, serrano, all the spices and salt. When the onion mixture is cool, add to the bowl. Gently combine without overworking. Divide into 4 thick burger patties.

Sear on a grill or in a grill pan until they reach desired temperature. Serve on your favorite kind of hamburger bun. Top with the chutney and aioli.

Prepare mango-cherry-chili chutney

In a skillet, melt butter and sauté onion and garlic until tender, 4 to 5 minutes. Add mango and chipotle, then mix in tomato paste and stir for about 2 minutes.

Add all remaining ingredients except the cilantro. Simmer over low heat for 30 to 40 minutes. Meanwhile, prepare an ice bath.

If the chutney becomes too dry, you may need to add ½ to 1 cup water and reduce some more. Mix and taste for balanced flavor of sweetness, acidity, spice and saltiness. When satisfied with the flavor, remove from heat and chill in the ice bath.

After chutney has cooled, add cilantro. Use to top 50/50 Bombay burgers or refrigerate for future use. It keeps for several months in an airtight container in the refrigerator.

Makes 4½ cups

✻ This chutney is awesome when eaten as a garnish with all types of curry dishes.

Caramelized Jerk Chicken

Apple, Onion and Brie Panini

Jerk chicken is so aromatic, with allspice, cinnamon and ginger. My daughter Ashley's favorite thing is apple pie with these same beautiful aromas. One day in the kitchen, she was helping me out because I was short-staffed. She said she had an idea for a lunch special and I said, "Go for it." So she slapped together this sandwich: butter-sautéed sweet apples, sweet Walla Walla onion, spicy jerk chicken and a slab of triple crème Brie between some really nice bread, then cooked it on a panini press. All I could say was, "OMG, Ashley! Why won't you stay in the kitchen? I need you."

SERVES FOUR

2 (8-ounce) chicken breasts, halved horizontally

4–6 tablespoons Jamaican Jerk Paste (page 135)

1½ cups sweet onion (Vidalia or Walla Walla),
   sliced lengthwise along the rib

3 tablespoons Herb Butter (page 27)

2 cups sliced apples, about ¼ inch thick

½ cup dark raisins

¼ teaspoon ground nutmeg

½ teaspoon ground cinnamon

¼ teaspoon ground allspice

1½ teaspoons sugar

1 tablespoon kosher salt

8–10 ounces Brie, cut into ¼-inch slices
   (it is not necessary to remove the rind)

4 panini buns, sliced open
   (can substitute ciabatta or baguette)

In a bowl, place chicken breasts and cover with Jerk Paste on both sides. Marinate in the refrigerator for 2 to 3 hours or overnight. Once chicken breasts have marinated sufficiently, let them come to room temperature before cooking.

In a skillet, sauté onion for 4 minutes in Herb Butter. Add apples and raisins and continue sautéing for 2 minutes. Add nutmeg, cinnamon, allspice, sugar and salt. Stir well.

Remove from heat, scrape onto a plate and return skillet to stove. Shake off some marinade from chicken and place the breasts in the hot pan, adding more butter if needed. Cook just until opaque.

Remove from heat and slice chicken thin on a bias. Build your sandwiches on the buns by layering chicken, onion mixture and Brie. Cook on a panini press or as you would a grilled cheese in a pan.

If you are not a spice lover, back off the amount of jerk seasoning. By adding a triple crème Brie, though, the fat in the cheese will cut the heat and so will the sweet of the apples, so you may actually find yourself adding a little more hot sauce!

Aiolis

I'm very fond of using aiolis—basically an emulsification of egg and oil, much like mayonnaise—to enhance sandwiches and appetizers. I even recommend swirling them in soups and sauces for extra depths of intensity. They're simple to make, once you get the hang of them, and it's easy to alter the flavor profile.

Here are the aiolis I use in the book, but feel free to invent your own! Always make sure your egg yolks are very cold and very fresh. Most of these aiolis keep for up to 2 weeks in an airtight container in the refrigerator; if you add fresh cheeses or other easily spoilable ingredients, they may only keep for about 10 days.

Basic Aioli

3 egg yolks

3 tablespoons freshly squeezed
 lemon juice

1 tablespoon apple cider vinegar

1 tablespoon kosher salt

⅛ teaspoon cayenne pepper

1½ cups canola-olive oil blend

In a blender, place all ingredients except oil. Attach the lid and blend for 2 minutes. As the machine continues to run, slowly drizzle in the oil through the hole in the lid. Once the consistency of mayonnaise, stop and scrape into an airtight container using a spatula. Do not overblend.

Use as an ingredient in the Homemade Russian Dressing (see "Jersey Style" Triple Decker Sloppy Joe, page 98) or as a condiment in the recipe of your choice.

Makes about 2 cups

Cumin Aioli

3 egg yolks

3 tablespoons freshly squeezed
 lemon juice

1 tablespoon apple cider vinegar

1 tablespoon kosher salt

⅛ teaspoon cayenne pepper

1 flat tablespoon ground cumin

1½ cups canola-olive oil blend

In a food processor, place all ingredients except oil. Attach the lid and blend for 2 minutes. As the machine continues to run, slowly drizzle in the oil through the hole in the lid. Once the consistency of mayonnaise, stop and scrape into an airtight container using a spatula. Do not overblend.

Use with the Sunrise Club España (page 122) or as a condiment in the recipe of your choice.

Makes 2 cups

Orange-Mustard Aioli

3 egg yolks
2 tablespoons Grey Poupon
    Dijon mustard
1 tablespoon orange zest
1 tablespoon kosher salt
2 tablespoons lemon juice
Pinch of cayenne pepper
1½ cups canola-olive oil blend

In a food processor, place all ingredients except oil. Attach the lid and blend for 2 minutes. As the machine continues to run, slowly drizzle in the oil through the hole in the lid. Once the consistency of mayonnaise, stop and scrape into an airtight container using a spatula. Do not overblend.

Use with the Mojo-Roasted Pulled Pork (page 116) or as a condiment in the recipe of your choice.

Makes about 1¾ cups

Roasted Garlic and Scotch Bonnet Aioli

3 egg yolks
½ cup roasted garlic (page 68)
½ teaspoon bottled
    Scotch bonnet hot sauce

Juice of 3 lemons
Dash of cayenne pepper
½ teaspoon salt and pepper
¾ cup vegetable oil

In a food processor, place all ingredients except oil. Attach the lid and blend for 2 minutes. As the machine continues to run, slowly drizzle in the oil through the hole in the lid. Once the consistency of mayonnaise, stop and scrape into an airtight container using a spatula. Do not overblend.

Use with the Cuban-Style Bacalao Fritters (page 48) or as a condiment in the recipe of your choice.

Makes 4 cups

Wasabi Aioli

2 tablespoons wasabi powder
2 tablespoons cold water
1 tablespoon soy sauce
2 tablespoons rice wine
3 egg yolks
1 teaspoon kosher salt
1 cup canola oil

In a small bowl, mix wasabi and water into a paste with a fork. Incorporate soy and mirin.

In a food processor, place egg yolks, wasabi mixture and salt. Attach the lid and blend for 2 minutes. As the machine continues to run, slowly drizzle in the oil through the hole in the lid. Once the consistency of mayonnaise, stop and scrape into an airtight container using a spatula. Do not overblend.

Use with the Jamaican Jerk-

Marinated and Seared Blue Fin Tuna (page 140) or as a condiment in the recipe of your choice.

Makes 1¾ cups

Chipotle Aioli or Goat Cheese-Chipotle Aioli

2 small cloves garlic
1 tablespoon kosher salt
¼ cup chopped cilantro
2 chipotle peppers in adobo sauce
3 tablespoons lemon juice
2 egg yolks
¾ cup light olive oil
3-ounce goat cheese log,
    room temperature
    (skip if preparing Chipotle Aioli)

In a food processor, pulse garlic, salt, cilantro, chipotle and lemon juice.

Add egg yolks, reattach the lid and continue to blend. As the machine continues to run, slowly drizzle in the oil through the hole in the lid. Once the consistency of mayonnaise, stop. Do not overblend.

Continue to next step if preparing Goat Cheese-Chipotle Aioli; otherwise, scrape into an airtight container using a spatula. Use Chipotle Aioli with the Crispy Fried Grouper (page 110) or as a condiment in the recipe of your choice.

Add goat cheese and pulse until just combined. Scrape into an airtight container using a spatula. Use on the 50/50 Bombay Burger (page 102) or as a condiment in the recipe of your choice.

Makes about 2 cups

Crispy Fried Grouper Sandwich

with Chipotle Aioli, Caramelized Sweet Onions, Lettuce and Tomato

It's not too often that I will eat fried foods without feeling guilty, but this is too good not to eat. When grouper season is open, I like to use black grouper because it is a nicely firm yet flaky fish. The light, crisp breading here also has lots of flavor. Fresh aioli blended with chile peppers gives this sandwich the ideal, balanced heat. Toast the bun, slather it with my recipe for Chipotle Aioli and take my advice—don't feel guilty at all.

SERVES TWO TO FOUR

4 tablespoons sesame oil

¼ cup teriyaki sauce

2 tablespoons lemon pepper

2½ pounds fresh grouper fillets, bloodlines removed

¾ cup garbanzo bean flour

½ cup all-purpose flour

¼ cup panko

2 tablespoons garlic powder

2 tablespoons onion powder

¼ teaspoon cayenne pepper

6 tablespoons butter

1 small, yellow onion, sliced on the rib

1 cup vegetable oil

2 (6-inch) baguettes

Chipotle Aioli (page 109)

2 iceberg or romaine lettuce leaves

4 slices vine-ripe tomato

In a large bowl, place sesame oil, teriyaki and lemon pepper and whisk well. Add fish, making sure to coat all sides with the marinade. Refrigerate for about 1 hour or overnight.

In another bowl, mix flours, panko, garlic powder, onion powder and cayenne. Set aside.

In a large skillet, melt butter and sauté onion over medium-high heat. Once golden brown and caramelized, remove onions from heat.

Remove the marinated fish fillets from the refrigerator and let any excess marinade drip off into the bowl. Place fillets in the dry flour mixture and coat evenly.

In a FryDaddy or large skillet, heat vegetable oil to 300°F and slowly drop the floured fish into the hot oil. Fry until crispy and golden brown. Place on paper towels to drain excess oil.

Slice baguettes and spread them with aioli. Then add fish and top with caramelized onions, lettuce and tomatoes. Slice into halves and serve.

For a little extra depth, Anchor New Zealand cheddar (if you can find it) is fantastic for melting or warming on this sandwich. If you can't find that, I suggest a cheese similar in high fat content.

Marinated Mahi-Mahi in Breadfruit Taco Shells

with Pico de Gallo and Cilantro Crema

This recipe was conceived in the Cayman Islands during breadfruit season with my executive chef at the time, Sara Mair. She and I were in the kitchen trying to think of some new dishes, and I had been making these pretty fried breadfruit bowls for our ceviche presentation. They looked beautiful, like crisp sunflowers. Sara came up with the idea of putting the breadfruit in a taco fryer we had bought a few weeks before and trying them as tacos. They became an instant hit; everyone loved these things. Best tacos ever! Even if you can't make the breadfruit shell, the marinated mahi-mahi and all the other elements that go inside are delicious too.

MAKES TWELVE TO FOURTEEN TACOS

1½ pounds fresh mahi-mahi, bloodline removed

2 teaspoons ground cumin

2 tablespoons ground coriander

Kosher salt and pepper, to taste

¾ cup extra virgin olive oil, divided

½ cup chopped parsley, divided

1 cup chopped cilantro, divided

1 cup brunoised yellow onion

2 cloves garlic, minced

2 serrano chilis, seeded and minced

1 can seasoned black beans, including liquid

1 large green breadfruit, skin on, washed,
    sliced very thin on a meat slicer

1 firm, ripe avocado, peeled, seeded, diced and salted

1 cup Pico de Gallo (page 164)

1 recipe Cilantro Crema (page 51)

4 limes, cut into quarters

Cut fish lengthwise into 3 or 4 strips. Then cut strips horizontally into small cubes.

Place fish in a bowl and toss with cumin, coriander, salt, pepper and ¼ cup olive oil. Toss in ¼ cup parsley and ¼ cup cilantro and mix. Set aside to marinate.

In a medium saucepot, heat ¼ cup olive oil over medium-high heat and sauté onions, garlic and serrano until onions are soft. Add black beans and their liquid. Bring to a simmer and cook for 2 to 3 minutes. Season to taste.

Transfer onion-bean mixture to a food processor. Pulse until fairly smooth. Pour into a bowl. Mix in remaining parsley and cilantro and set aside.

In a sauté pan, add remaining olive oil, heat over high and sauté the marinated fish strips until opaque. Season with salt and pepper to taste, remove from heat, and set aside.

Prepare a professional fryer with a deep, taco-shape basket. Heat oil to 300°F. Place breadfruit slices into the fry basket and fry until golden brown. Remove from basket and drain on paper towels.

In the bottom crease of each taco shell, place a few spoonfuls of black bean puree. Add about 2 ounces cooked fish, then 2 teaspoons each of salted avocado and pico de gallo. Finish with crema and serve immediately with lime wedges.

❋ The breadfruit tacos can only be made if you have a professional deep fryer and if you can find fresh breadfruit, which is not too easy in most parts of the world. So if you are presented with these obstacles, just purchase store-bought taco shells or use the above fish recipe to make a burrito or quesadilla. If you do have the opportunity to attempt making breadfruit taco shells, however, the experience is well worth the effort.

Grilled Nectarine, Prosciutto, Arugula and Feta Cheese

on Ciabatta Bread with Ginger-Almond Butter

Summer's stone-fruit season rolls around and I can't help but think of this sandwich, which is really amazing with the firm, ripe-but-crisp nectarines added to it. Indeed, this sandwich satisfies all of your taste buds. You have the salt from the feta cheese and prosciutto, the sweet from the nectarines, the piquancy from the arugula, and a nice, buttery bite from the ginger-almond butter. Topped off with the crunch of the ciabatta, this sandwich is hands down one of my favorites.

MAKES TWO SANDWICHES

2 sandwich-size ciabatta rolls, sliced in half
8 tablespoons Ginger-Almond Butter (page 27)
2 handfuls baby arugula
4 tablespoons olive oil, divided, plus more for brushing
3–4 ounces Greek feta in olive oil,
    cut into ¼-inch slices
2 firm ripe nectarines, cut into ¼-inch slices
¼ pound imported, shaved prosciutto

Butter all sides of ciabatta rolls with 2 tablespoons butter each.

In a small bowl, toss arugula with 2 tablespoons olive oil.

Heat a cast-iron skillet or a grill pan on high. Add remaining oil. Once hot, char cheese and nectarines on one side, about 2 minutes, then flip and do the same to the other sides.

Layer fruit and cheese on the bottoms of the open rolls. Add prosciutto to the sandwiches, then top with arugula. Close sandwiches and brush with a little extra olive oil. Briefly grill on the skillet or heat on a panini press.

❋ This sandwich is best enjoyed in the summer during stone-fruit season when nectarines, plums and peaches are at their peak. Mangos could be used as well. All of these fruits work beautifully in this sandwich. The key is making sure the fruits are crisp, not too soft or overripe. Also, use a good-quality feta from a gourmet cheese purveyor rather than a packaged feta from the grocery store.

Mojo-Roasted Pulled Pork

with Citrus-Zested Pickled Onions
in Twice-Fried Yucca "Tostones" Sandwiches

Given that I have restaurants in tropical places like Miami, Grand Cayman and Harbour Island, Bahamas, I have always had access to fresh yucca—one of my favorite tubers to eat. Like many Latin American and Caribbean people, I enjoy preparing them in a number of ways. One day, I took a couple of pieces of very soft, boiled yucca, sliced them horizontally and tossed them in the fryer until they were golden brown. I blotted off the extra oil and then fried them again. Once I had filled those extra-crispy things with the pork and pickled onions, they made for the most amazing sandwich!

MAKES TWO SANDWICHES

Mojo-Roasted Pulled Pork

1 (7–10 pound) pork butt
5 cloves garlic
1 recipe Mojo Marinade (page 159)
Salt and pepper, to taste

Twice-Fried Yucca "Tostones" Sandwich

4 pieces salted, boiled yucca, about
   4 inches long and 1½ inches thick
2 cups vegetable oil
Salt and pepper, to taste
1 ounce Orange Mustard Aioli (page 109)
6 ounces cooked Mojo-Roasted Pulled Pork
2 ounces Citrus-Zested Pickled Onions (page 183)

continued on page 118

continued from page 116

Prepare mojo-roasted pulled pork

With a knife, slit pork in five different places and stud with whole garlic cloves. Rub pork with marinade, and let marinate overnight in the refrigerator.

Preheat oven to 375°F.

Remove pork from refrigerator and season all over with salt and pepper to taste.

Place pork on a roasting rack and roast until internal temperature reaches 155°F. Remove from oven and let rest until cool. Then pull pork apart into chunks with your fingers, removing and discarding overly fatty pieces along the way.

Prepare twice-fried yucca "tostones" sandwiches

In a deep skillet or FryDaddy, heat oil to 300°F.

Make sure the core of the yucca has been removed from the center of the tubers. Place each piece, one by one, into the hot oil. Once yuccas are golden brown, remove them with a slotted spoon and place on paper towels to blot off excess oil.

Using a kitchen mallet, smash each yucca into a flat rectangular slab, about ¼ inch thick. It will not be a perfect rectangle, but try to get all slabs uniform in size. Now drop them in the hot oil for a second fry, cooking until just a bit more golden brown. Remove from oil, blot on paper towels and season with salt and pepper.

Spread each yucca rectangle with aioli. On 2 pieces, place generous portions of pulled pork. Add onions and top with remaining yucca pieces.

Imported, sliced Manchego, melted or simply added to this, also adds fantastic flavor. Enjoy with an ice-cold beer of your choice—it goes fabulously with the fried element of the sandwich and cuts through the fat.

Open-Faced Cherry Wood-Smoked Tuna Salad

This tuna sandwich takes quite a bit more time than simply opening a can of fish and draining it, but it is well worth the trouble. I like to melt Reading cheddar cheese over this, which is a lot like Emmental: It's nutty in flavor and spreads out evenly when exposed to heat. It's a perfect match for the cherry wood smoke, bringing out the meaty texture of the fresh tuna. However, it can be difficult to find in your usual market, so look for quality substitutions, such as the aforementioned Emmental, or Cabot clothbound.

MAKES FOUR SANDWICHES

2 pounds fresh tuna steaks,
   bloodlines removed, cut into 4 steaks
¼ cup olive oil
2 tablespoons sea salt
2 tablespoons garlic powder
2 tablespoons onion powder
1–2 cups cherry wood chips
   (can substitute alder or mesquite wood)
Water, for soaking
2–4 tablespoons Rémoulade
   (depending on how moist you like your tuna) (page 51)
4 slices country white bread, or your favorite bread
4–8 ounces grated Reading cheese
   (depending on how much cheese you like;
   can substitute any cheese you like)

Rub tuna steaks with olive oil. Sprinkle with the seasonings and set aside.

Prior to smoking, soak chips for 30 minutes.

Smoke until tuna is opaque throughout. Remove from heat.

Once cool enough to handle, crumble tuna into a bowl. Refrigerate until at least room temperature. Mix in rémoulade.

Build open-face sandwiches by dividing tuna mixture evenly among bread slices. Top with grated cheese and melt under broiler until bubbly.

❋ On a chilly day, enjoy this with a cup of Roasted Tomato-Kaffir Lime Leaf Bisque with Goat Cheese Ice (page 34).

Sunrise Club España

Delius gets up at the crack of dawn to play golf so he can be finished in time to make it to the restaurant for lunch service. His buddies used to whine and moan about the 6:37 a.m. tee time—until I started getting up at 5:30 and making them brown-bag sandwiches. Now, each one receives one of these foil-wrapped sandwiches with a semifrozen drink pack. You know the saying "The way to a man's heart is through his stomach"? Well, in this case, it's through his stomach *and* onto the golf course.

MAKES FOUR SANDWICHES

8 strips Vande Rose Farms uncured bacon,
   or another favorite brand
8 large eggs
Freshly cracked pepper and kosher salt
5½ ounces thinly sliced Serrano ham
   (can substitute prosciutto)
4 ounces Manchego cheese, cut into 8 slices
3 ounces Cumin Aioli (page 108)
4 round brioche buns

In a nonstick skillet over high heat, cook bacon. After it crisps on one side, turn over and crisp on the other. Remove and place on paper towels to blot off excess grease.

Without breaking the yolks, crack eggs into the hot bacon grease, then season. Cook to desired doneness, flipping once. As soon as you've flipped, place 1 slice cheese on each egg.

Turn off burner and slice each bun open. Spread aioli on inner sides of buns. Divide ham equally among buns.

On top of ham, layer 2 cooked eggs and bacon on each sandwich. Add top halves of buns and enjoy.

✳ Make sure the bacon and Manchego are high quality. Splurge on this one! It's nice to sauté some fresh vine-ripe tomatoes in a little olive oil, salt and pepper to add to this sandwich too.

CHAPTER 5

SEA FA

I have always been drawn to the sea and its wonderful (and wonderful-tasting) inhabitants. Maybe it's because of my astrological nature—I'm a Cancer—but more likely, it's because of my grandfather. As a little girl, I spent almost every vacation in the Florida Panhandle at my Ma and Pa's house on Santa Rosa Sound. My Pa would take me out before daylight on his little skiff to meet the shrimp boats, and we would fill our 5-gallon bucket with live, jumping shrimp for a measly five bucks. When daylight broke, we would get on our sneakers and gather up the bay scallops, with their beautiful iridescent eyes, that were swimming backward on the sandbar. We would clean them and then head inside for breakfast. Pa would cook the most perfect bacon-basted sunny-side-up eggs I have ever tasted to go with those sweet cornmeal-fried shrimp and scallops. It was way back then that I learned how to cook the freshest of seafood and fish, using only the most basic herbs, spices and seasonal produce.

Caribbean Steamed Fish One Pot

with Green Bananas, Malanga, Jamaican Yellow Yam, Calabaza and Vine-Ripe Tomatoes

Just as the name suggests, this dish is all cooked in one large pot. Cast iron is best, but if not available, you can use a large, deep skillet. This is a dish that I have tasted on many different islands, where each one has its own unique version and name. Here are the ingredients I like in mine—they're simple, fresh and healthy.

SERVES FOUR

2 green bananas

4 tablespoons salted butter

1 cup finely diced onion

4 cloves garlic, crushed and chopped

2 tablespoons tomato paste

1½ cups white wine

2 cups clam broth

1 can coconut milk, or 1½ cups fresh coconut milk
 (page 168)

12 wedges calabaza, 3–4 inches long, skin on
 (substitute kabocha squash or Caribbean pumpkin)

1 cup peeled and diced Jamaican yellow yam

2 cups peeled and large-diced malanga

2 ears corn, kernels cut off cob

2 cups diced vine-ripe tomatoes

12 allspice berries, whole

¼ cup fresh thyme leaves

1 Scotch bonnet chili pepper,
 seeded and chopped fine

Salt and pepper, to taste

4 (8-ounce) fresh snapper or hogfish fillets
 (substitute any white, flaky fish)
 2 tablespoons Clarified Butter (page 27)

Slit skin of banana lengthwise without cutting into banana flesh. In a pot of boiling, salted water, cook the skin-on bananas for 20 to 25 minutes. The incision made in the skin will widen after cooking, allowing peeling with ease once bananas are drained and cooled. Slice the cooled bananas horizontally into ½-inch-thick slices and reserve.

Place a cast-iron pot over low heat and melt salted butter. Sauté onions and garlic until a little soft. Add tomato paste and stir, cooking for 1 to 2 minutes. Add wine and simmer for 2 minutes more. Add clam broth and coconut milk and return to a simmer.

Add calabaza, yam, malanga, corn, reserved banana, tomato, allspice, thyme and Scotch bonnet. Season to taste with salt and pepper. Simmer for 10 to 15 minutes, until vegetables are fork-tender.

Meanwhile, season fish fillets on both sides with salt and pepper. Heat a sauté pan with clarified butter and add fillets, skin side down. When edges begin to turn golden brown, flip fillets and sear the other side, about 3 minutes. When fillets are just opaque through (still slightly undercooked in the center), remove from heat. Divide broth and vegetables among 4 large bowls and top with fillets, skin side up. Garnish and serve immediately.

Cumin- and Coriander- Dusted Mahi-Mahi

with Eggplant and Vine-Ripe Tomato Sauté, Slivered Garlic and Sambal Pepper Sauce, Topped with Cilantro Crema

This bright and eye-pleasing dish started with inspiration from one of my first chefs de cuisine, Mary Rohan. Then I changed it up by making my own sambal and adding homemade clam juice. If you're short on time, you can purchase sambal and clam juice at the market. Or you could make the sambal a couple of days ahead of time. It is well worth the effort in the end.

SERVES EIGHT

Cumin- and Coriander-Dusted Mahi-Mahi

¼ cup Clarified Butter (page 27)

3 pounds fresh mahi-mahi, bloodlines removed and cut into 8 (6-ounce) portions of equal thickness

2 tablespoons ground coriander

2 tablespoons kosher salt

1 tablespoon ground cumin

1 recipe Sambal Pepper Sauce (page 165)

1 recipe Cilantro Crema (page 51)

Eggplant and Vine-Ripe Tomato Sauté

3 cups diced eggplant

Juice of 2 lemons

4 tablespoons kosher salt

½ cup extra-virgin olive oil

4–6 cloves garlic, sliced thin

1½ cups diced yellow onion

1 tablespoon toasted ground coriander

1 teaspoon toasted ground cumin

¾ cup white wine

1 cup Homemade Clam Juice (see below)

3 cups seeded and diced vine-ripe tomatoes

⅛ cup Sambal Pepper Sauce, plus more if you like spice (page 165) but add at the end after tasting

2 bunches cilantro, chopped

continued on page 130

Homemade Clam Juice

4 tablespoons butter

½ cup chopped onion

½ cup chopped garlic

½ cup chopped celery

½ cup chopped carrot

2 pounds middle neck clams, rinsed

2 bay leaves

6 black peppercorns

In a skillet, melt butter and make a mirepoix by sautéing onions, garlic, celery and carrots until fragrant. Remove from heat and set aside.

In a large pot, place clams. Cover with water. Add mirepoix, bay leaves and peppercorns. Boil for 15 minutes, strain and reduce to 1 to 2 cups. Remove clams from shells and dip into melted butter for a snack.

continued from page 129

Prepare mahi-mahi

Preheat oven to 400°F. Season mahi-mahi fillets on both sides with the spices.

In a large skillet over high heat, heat clarified butter. Sear fish until golden brown, about 2 minutes, then flip over and cook for about 2 minutes more.

Transfer to a baking sheet and finish cooking in the oven until just cooked through, about 4 minutes.

Once fish is cooked, place about ½ cup of eggplant sauté in the middle of the plates. Place the cooked fillets on top and then garnish with cilantro crema.

✳ If the fillets are 1 inch or thinner, the cooking process can be completed in the skillet.

Prepare eggplant and tomato sauté

Toss eggplant with lemon juice and 2 tablespoons salt. Set aside.

In a skillet, heat olive oil on medium-high heat. Sauté garlic and onion until fork-tender.

Add eggplant and sauté for 5 to 10 minutes.

Add coriander, cumin, wine and clam juice and simmer for 5 minutes. Add tomatoes and sambal. Let simmer for about 10 minutes.

Season with remaining kosher salt. Cool in an ice bath. Once cool, add chopped cilantro. Heat before serving.

✳ This dish is also wonderful served with swordfish or Chilean sea bass, as the eggplant really stands up to an oilier fish.

Lemon-Chili Yellowtail Snapper

with Ginger, Bok Choy and Julienned Seasonal Vegetables

I'm always brainstorming fresh ideas for my Saturday interactive cooking classes held at Ortanique on the Mile. We have a lot of repeat attendees, so teaching new dishes every month is a must. The classes are a blast to teach and, judging from the feedback, even more fun to attend. They also have become a terrific testing ground for my recipes, as the dishes need to be easy to execute as well as creative and conducive to cooking at home. This one was a big hit.

SERVES SIX

6 (6-ounce) portions yellowtail snapper, skin on
Salt, pepper and flour, for dusting
¼ cup olive oil
2 cups scallions, finely julienned lengthwise
¼ cup fresh ginger, finely julienned lengthwise
½ cup chopped cilantro
1 cup julienned red pepper
1 cup julienned yellow pepper
2 cups julienned baby bok choy*
2 cups Lemon-Chili Sauce

Lemon-Chili Sauce

5 ounces freshly squeezed lemon juice
1 ounce yuzu (optional)
½ cup soy sauce
3 tablespoons black vinegar
¼ cup fish sauce
3 tablespoons sugar
3 tablespoons minced garlic
¼ cup sweet chili garlic sauce, store-bought
1 tablespoon sea salt
1 cup grapeseed oil

* Feel free to add whatever Asian vegetables—pak choi, Chinese cabbage, lotus root—that you can find in season in your local stores.

continued on page 134

continued from page 132

Prepare yellowtail snapper

Preheat oven to 500°F.

Season with salt and pepper on both sides, dust with flour, and set aside on platter.

In a large skillet over medium-high heat, place oil. Add seasoned fish, skin side down. Using a large spatula, press down on fish if they begin to curl. Cook until golden brown, about 2 minutes, then flip over and do the same to the other side. Transfer fish to a baking sheet, but reserve the pan with the cooking juices.

Place fish in oven and cook until opaque all the way through, 5 to 8 minutes, depending on the thickness.

Meanwhile, reheat the fish skillet over medium-high heat. When hot, sauté scallions, ginger, cilantro, red and yellow peppers, and bok choy together quickly. Pour in Lemon-Chili Sauce and remove from heat.

Remove fish from oven and divide evenly among 6 dinner plates. Using tongs, pile vegetables on top of each piece of fish. Divide remaining pan juices among the plates, drizzling over fish. I also recommend adding ½ cup of jasmine rice to each plate if desired.

 Ask your fishmonger to cut the fillets into the proper-size portions for you.

Prepare lemon-chili sauce

In a food processor, place all ingredients except the grapeseed oil. Pulse the machine to combine. Keep machine running and slowly add oil until the mixture has emulsified.

Set aside for use with the Lemon-Chili Yellowtail Snapper.

Makes about 2 cups

European Branzino Niçoise

with Haricots Verts, Caper Berries, Teardrop Tomatoes and Butter-Poached Gold Potatoes

Branzino is one of my all-time favorite fishes. You will need to find this in a real fishmonger's market, not a grocery store, as most won't carry it. (Unless you have one that you trust, I don't recommend buying your fish at a grocery store anyway, as it's hardly ever fresh.) To accompany this fish, which has a stronger flavor than many of the more tropical fishes that I frequently highlight in my fare, I have incorporated the boldness of olives and capers. Swapping it with a fresh seared tuna steak would complement this preparation perfectly. Pair this dish with a great Tempranillo, close your eyes and taste the Mediterranean.

SERVES SIX

1 cup extra virgin olive oil, divided
1 small onion, brunoised
10 cloves garlic, sliced thin
¾ cup coarsely chopped small capers
½ cup coarsely chopped pitted kalamata olives
3 fresh marinated anchovy fillets, minced (optional)
2 pints grape or teardrop tomatoes, halved lengthwise
2 large bunches basil, blanched, leaves only
2 tablespoons good-quality balsamic vinegar
2 tablespoons Dijon mustard
Kosher salt and freshly cracked pepper, to taste
6 (7-ounce) fresh branzino fillets, skin on,
*   pin bones removed*
¼ cup cooking oil
¾ stick salted butter
½ cup water
6 medium, thin-skinned, new potatoes,
*   sliced and blanched*
1 pound haricots verts, stems removed and blanched

In a skillet, heat ⅓ cup olive oil. Sauté onion and garlic until tender. Remove from heat and place in a medium stainless-steel bowl. Place in the refrigerator to cool to room temperature.

When cooled, remove from refrigerator and add capers, olives, tomatoes and anchovies (optional). Toss. Add blanched basil leaves and mix gently.

In a separate small bowl, whisk together balsamic vinegar and mustard. Slowly drizzle in the remaining olive oil while continuously whisking. Still whisking, slowly and evenly pour over the tomato mixture. Season with salt and pepper. Toss gently and set aside.

Dry off the skin of the fish fillets and sprinkle both sides with salt and pepper.

In a large skillet over medium-high heat, place cooking oil. Add fish fillets, skin side down, and

Continued on page 138

continued from page 136

cook until golden brown around the edges, then flip. Make sure not to flip too quickly.

Reduce heat to low and continue cooking. Branzino fillets are typically thin, so after you have flipped them over they may only need 2 or 3 minutes more to finish cooking.

Meanwhile, heat another large skillet over medium-high heat and melt butter. Add water.

Place potato rounds in a single layer and simmer until liquid has been reduced by half. Heat haricots verts by placing on top of the potatoes. When all liquid has evaporated and potatoes' edges are golden brown, remove from heat.

On the center of each of 6 dinner plates, place 4 potato discs flat. Divide haricots verts evenly among plates, placing next to potatoes. Top them with a fish fillet, skin side up. Top fish with about ½ cup tomato mixture and some of its juices. Serve while still warm.

*This recipe calls for several elements to be blanched. The best way to do that is to quickly dunk ingredients in boiling salted water, then remove and plunge them immediately into an ice bath. Then drain them, or dry on paper towels, so they don't get soggy.

Jamaican Jerk Paste-Marinated and Seared Bluefin Tuna

with Papaya-Mango Salsa and Wasabi Aioli

I decided to marinate this tuna in jerk seasoning, breaking tradition from encrusting it in sesame seeds, a method we all know and love—and that is perhaps just the tiniest bit overused. Adding the salsa of fresh mango and papaya simultaneously enhances and cools down the jerk spices. Because this preparation is from outside the box, it's still one of Delius' favorite dishes from any of our restaurants. It also became a winner on the menu and is one of those dishes our patrons will not allow us to remove.

SERVES SIX

6 (8-ounce) tuna steaks, center cut, sushi quality
6 tablespoons Jamaican Jerk Paste (page 145)
2 tablespoons canola-olive oil blend
1 cup Wasabi Aioli (page 109)
2 cups Papaya-Mango Salsa (page 163)

Place tuna steaks in a stainless-steel bowl. Coat steaks with Jamaican Jerk Paste. Marinate in the refrigerator for at least 2 hours or overnight.

Prepare either a hot grill or a hot skillet, according to your preference, and add oil. Cook tuna on medium-high heat on the grill or over high heat in the skillet for about 2 minutes on each side, until seared. The temperature of the tuna should be rare.

Drizzle or paint 6 dinner plates with little swirls of Wasabi Aioli. Place fillets on top with a garnish of Papaya-Mango Salsa. Pour extra Wasabi Aioli into ramekins for dipping.

✳ Ask a fishmonger whom you trust to cut the tuna steaks. Sashimi-quality tuna is a must. Because the tuna is only seared on the outside, then sliced thin and presented on an oblong platter, it makes quite a statement as a Caribbean-style tuna tataki.

Seasonal Pan-Seared Black Grouper
with Buttered Chayote and Carrots in a Bacardi Limón Sauce

I created this dish back in the days of Norma's on the Beach. It has been my signature fish dish since 1996. Customers will simply not allow this dish to be removed from my core menu. Recognizing the depleted grouper population and out of respect for grouper season, when moratoriums on fishing are in place, however, I change out the fish accordingly.

SERVES SIX

Seasonal Pan-Seared Black Grouper
¼ cup chopped fresh garlic
½ cup teriyaki sauce
4 tablespoons sesame oil
2 tablespoons lemon pepper, plus more to taste
2½ pounds fresh black grouper, bloodlines removed, portioned into 6 equal fillets (substitute mahi-mahi when grouper is not in season)
4 tablespoons oil
2 tablespoons salted butter
2 cups julienned chayote
2 cups julienned carrots

Bacardi Limón Sauce
1 stick salted butter
3 cups peeled and coarsely sliced yellow onions
1 cup Bacardi Limón
½ cup teriyaki sauce
1½ cups hot pepper jelly
2 cups water

Prepare fish
Preheat oven to 350°F.

In a stainless-steel bowl, mix garlic, teriyaki, sesame oil and lemon pepper together with a whisk. Place the fish fillets in the mixture to marinate. Cover and refrigerate until the sauce is ready.

Prepare Bacardi Limón sauce
In a medium saucepan, melt butter. Sauté onions until they turn a deep caramel color (but don't let them burn and become bitter). Add Bacardi Limón and simmer for about 5 minutes over medium-low heat.

Add teriyaki, jelly and water. Bring to a boil, then reduce heat to medium. Simmer for 10 minutes.

Remove from heat and pour into a blender. Carefully blend into a caramel-colored glaze.

Makes about 2 quarts

continued on page 144

continued from page 142

Finish fish

Once the sauce has been prepared, finish cooking the fish. In a large skillet, heat oil on high. Place fillets in skillet, 3 at a time, without overcrowding the pan, and pan-sear to a golden brown, then flip and do the same to the other side. Place on a baking sheet and prepare remaining fillets. Transfer fillets to oven and cook for 8 to 10 minutes, until opaque.

Meanwhile, melt butter in a sauté pan. Lightly sauté chayote and carrots. Season with lemon pepper to taste.

Remove fish from oven and rest each fillet over Boniato-Sweet Plantain Mash (page 194), then pour 4 tablespoons sauce over each piece. Partner each fillet with chayote and carrots on the side and serve.

Mesquite Coffee and Cocoa Rub

3 tablespoons McCormick
    mesquite seasoning
3 tablespoons medium-roast coffee,
    finely ground as if for a drip maker
1 tablespoon semidark chocolate
    cocoa powder
1 tablespoon kosher salt

In a bowl, combine all ingredients.
    Makes ½ cup
✱I like this rub on my Domestic Rack
of Lamb in Amarena Cherry-Chipotle
Demi-Glace (page 206), but it's also
fantastic on short ribs, pork, steak
and, believe it or not, salmon.

Cumin and Coriander Spice Rub

2 tablespoons ground toasted cumin
2 tablespoons ground toasted
    coriander
1 tablespoon ground toasted
    fennel seed
1 tablespoon smoked paprika
2 tablespoons kosher salt

In a bowl, combine all ingredients.
    Makes ½ cup
✱This rub stands up beautifully to
short ribs and doesn't get lost when
you braise the meat, but it's also
extremely appealing on fish, such
as the Cumin- and Coriander-Dusted
Mahi-Mahi (page 128).

Jamaican Jerk Paste

¼ cup Jamaican allspice berries
2 teaspoons grated whole nutmeg
1 teaspoon cinnamon
4 Scotch bonnet chili peppers
    (remove seeds for less heat)
½ small red onion
1 cup scallions

Rubs and Pastes

(green & white parts), chopped
10 cloves garlic
1 (2-inch) piece fresh ginger, chopped
½ cup fresh thyme leaves
3 tablespoons brown sugar
4 tablespoons soy sauce
½ cup apple cider vinegar
Juice of ¼ lime
2 tablespoons kosher salt
½ cup olive oil

In a blender, place all ingredients
except olive oil. Cover and turn on
low speed. You may need to turn off,
remove the lid, stir and blend again
on a slightly higher speed.

Slowly drizzle in oil and continue
to pulse until mixture becomes a
paste. Using a spatula, scrape paste
into a glass Mason jar and store in
refrigerator.

The paste can be made ahead of
time and, refrigerated, will keep for
several weeks.
    Makes 2½ cups
✱Wear gloves when preparing the
jerk paste or marinating.
✱The paste is excellent for rubbing
into poultry, pork, beef and even
roasted potatoes. When using the
paste, remember that fish generally
needs less time marinating as it is a
more delicate protein than a meat.
For instance, when marinating the
Jamaican Jerk Paste-Marinated and
Seared Bluefin Tuna (page 140), you
will need the minimum amount of
time, 2 hours. You can then roast
your protein on a spit over a grill on
low heat until cooked, or roast it in
the oven at 350°F for the recommended cooking time.

Pan-Roasted Atlantic Swordfish and Rock Shrimp

with Sweet Corn, Andouille Sausage, New Potatoes and Carrots in Smoked Tomato Creole Sauce

In my restaurants and outside of them too, I hear many people comment about their dislike for swordfish. They say, "It's dry and fishy." And they're right. It is, if you don't buy fresh swordfish or if you overcook it. Swordfish should be cooked until slightly pink inside. By the time you sauce the steak and serve it, the heat from the exterior should reach the interior and finish cooking the steak perfectly. When you cut into it, juice should be running out of it. As for this particular sauce, I thicken it with masa harina (very finely ground cornmeal that is soaked in lime) instead of flour, so it's lighter than you might think, and it goes quite well with the meaty texture of fresh swordfish. Afterward, it can also be turned into a seafood chowder just by adding seafood of any type and extra clam stock. It's a great way to improve any leftovers you might have!

SERVES SIX

Pan-Roasted Atlantic Swordfish and Rock Shrimp

6 (8-ounce) fresh swordfish steaks
1 pound rock shrimp (frozen is fine)
Salt and pepper, to taste
¼ cup canola-olive oil blend

Smoked Tomato Creole Sauce

Cherry wood chips, soaked and drained, for smoking
12 plum tomatoes, smoked
1 (14.5-ounce) can crushed tomatoes
3 ears corn
¼ cup Herb Butter (page 27)
½ cup sliced garlic

2 onions, diced (about 1½ cups)
1 cup diced celery
1 cup finely diced carrots
2 pounds small new red potatoes, skin on, cut in half
2 cups diced Andouille sausage
1 tablespoon smoked paprika
2 teaspoons ground coriander
½ teaspoon cayenne pepper
2 tablespoons kosher salt
¼ cup masa harina
1 cup white wine
3 cups clam stock
½ cup fresh thyme leaves

continued on page 148

continued from page 146

Prepare swordfish and rock shrimp

Preheat oven to 400°F. Season swordfish steaks on both sides with salt and pepper. Place rock shrimp in a small bowl and season.

In a skillet, heat oil until very hot. Sear swordfish until golden brown, about 2 minutes. Flip over and do the same to the other side.

Remove from skillet and place in an ovenproof tray. Cook in oven for 4 to 5 minutes, until fish has turned opaque, with the flesh inside retaining a slight tinge of pink. Remove and let rest.

In the same skillet, sauté shrimp for about 2 minutes, until the shrimp turn opaque.

Place swordfish in the middle of a plate (I like to place it on hot white rice) and top with the sauce. Sprinkle with rock shrimp as a garnish and serve.

Prepare smoked tomato creole sauce

Download and consult directions from the Internet on how to smoke corn and tomatoes. Then prepare a grill or smoker outside in a well-ventilated area. Set tomatoes and corn to smoke over cherry wood chips. Be aware that this entire process may take up to a couple of hours. I recommend smoking for 30 to 45 minutes, depending on how heavy you want the smoke flavor.

Prepare 1 recipe Herb Butter (page 27).

In a 14-quart braiser pan, melt butter. Add garlic and onion and sauté for 5 minutes.

Add celery, carrots, potatoes, sausage, spices and salt and continue sautéing for 5 minutes. Add masa harina, stirring away the lumps.

Add wine and simmer for 1 minute while stirring continuously. Add clam stock and allow the mixture to simmer.

Remove tomatoes and corn from the smoker or grill and allow them to cool enough to handle. Seed tomatoes as best you can and dice. Cut corn from the cobs. Add tomatoes and corn to the sauce and continue cooking on a low simmer for about 20 minutes.

If you feel the sauce is too thin, transfer about 1½ cups to a blender. Blend on low speed and pour back into the sauce. Do not add more masa harina or any kind of thickener. Season to taste. Stir in thyme right before serving to preserve the color.

Makes about 2 quarts

Red Snapper Escovitch

with Carrots, Vidalia Onion, Allspice, Fresh Thyme, and Scotch Bonnet, Red and Yellow Peppers

Also known as *escabeche* or *escoveech*, this dish is common in many parts of the world. Whether it is a version from Spain, Portugal, Italy or Jamaica, it involves vinegar and/or citrus juices and vegetables. This recipe is a Jamaican version, where it is usually a traditional breakfast dish served at room temperature. At our restaurants, we offer it at lunch or dinner, usually as a whole fried fish covered in pickled veggies. Although it makes for a lovely presentation, frying a whole fish would be a bit difficult to prepare in a household kitchen, so in this recipe I call for fish fillets.

SERVES SIX

Red Snapper
6 (8-ounce) fresh red snapper fillets, skin on
   (substitute swordfish, halibut or cod)
2 tablespoons kosher salt
1 tablespoon freshly ground black pepper
4 tablespoons flour
½ cup canola oil

Escovitch Sauce
¼ cup olive-canola oil blend
¼ cup chopped garlic
2 cups sliced (along the onion rib) Vidalia
   or sweet yellow onions
10 allspice berries
1 Scotch bonnet chili pepper, seeded and sliced thin

2 cups julienned carrots
1 cup julienned chayote
4 tablespoons flour
4–5 tablespoons sugar
½ cup apple cider vinegar
1½ cups clam juice
1 large yellow Holland pepper, seeded and julienned
1 large red Holland pepper, seeded and julienned
1 tablespoon kosher salt
1 bunch fresh thyme leaves

Prepare snapper
Rinse and dry snapper fillets. Season both sides with salt and pepper and dust with flour. Set aside until sauce is ready.

continued on page 152

continued from page 150

Then, in a large, deep skillet, heat oil. Once hot, add fillets, skin side down. Cook fish over high heat for about 4 minutes, until golden brown and crispy. Flip over and cook for about 4 minutes more, until fillets are opaque throughout. Do not overcook.

Place fillets on dinner plates with Jamaican Rice and Peas (page 193). Spoon escovitch over fillets and serve.

Prepare escovitch

In a large skillet, heat oil on high. When hot, add garlic, onions, allspice and Scotch bonnet. Sauté until onions are halfway cooked. Add carrots and chayote and sauté for 5 minutes over medium heat.

Add flour, sugar, salt, vinegar and clam juice, stirring quickly. At this point, the mix will begin to thicken. Add Holland peppers and thyme. Continue simmering over low heat for about 4 minutes, while snapper is cooking.

When ready to serve, simmer sauce for 2 to 3 minutes, then remove from heat. Pour over cooked fish fillets.

Makes 2 quarts

❋ Escovitch sauce is also excellent on shrimp, swordfish or wahoo and, if you are a vegetarian or just would prefer a cold salad, it would be terrific over plain tofu or boiled green bananas.

CHAPTER 6

When deciding which recipes I wanted to include in my poultry chapter, I needed to think about a variety of birds and the endless methods of preparation. I wanted to choose recipes for those birds that are most commonly found and used in the average household. Instead of using exotic birds such as ostrich, partridge, squab or pheasant, I have chosen to use chicken, game hen, turkey and duck, seasoning them with the exotic flavors of a "Cuisine of the Sun." That is, the ethnic herbs and spices I gather in my travels, cooking with the locals of the different countries I am so fortunate to be able to experience.

Brown Stew Game Hens

This recipe is a bit like fricasseed chicken, except I have chosen to make a brown stew sauce separately from making it in the pot with the stewing bird. Preparing them separately allows the Cornish game hens' texture to remain moist and crispy-skinned as opposed to the stringiness that stewing sometimes causes. I marinate the game hens overnight and then cook them, pouring the heated sauce on them upon serving. The tamarind in this sauce adds a tart sweetness that gives this dish its Caribbean flair and helps balance the heat in the jerk seasoning.

SERVES FOUR

Game Hens

¾ cup Easy Jerk Chicken Marinade (page 159)
2 whole Cornish game hens
Kosher salt and black pepper, to taste
4 tablespoons Clarified Butter (page 27)

Brown Stew Sauce

6 tablespoons Herb Butter (page 27)
2 cups sliced yellow onion
8 cloves garlic, chopped
½ cup tamarind paste
1½ tablespoons sugar
1½ cups white wine
2 cups vine-ripe tomatoes, chopped
¾ cup Busha Browne's Planters Steak Sauce
  (available in most gourmet stores)
4 cups chicken stock
1 bunch thyme, tied with butcher's twine
4 tablespoons kosher salt
1 cup chopped scallions, green parts only

Prepare game hens

Remove game hens from the packaging. If they have giblets and necks, reserve them, along with the bones you remove from the birds, to fortify the chicken stock used in the Brown Stew Sauce.

Deboning a game hen or chicken may take some practice to perfect, but it lessens the cooking time by quite a bit. (It is best to watch a YouTube instructional video on deboning birds.)

After birds are deboned, split them in half. Place in a container with marinade and season with salt and pepper. Cover, refrigerate and let marinate for at least 2 hours or overnight.

Preheat oven to 450°F.

In a skillet large enough to hold all 4 splits of the game hens, heat butter. Remove hens from marinade and let the excess drip off into the container. Once butter is hot, add hens, skin side down. Lower heat to medium-high and crisp skin to a nice golden brown, 2 to 4 minutes. Flip and continue cooking for 1 minute more.

continued on page 158

continued from page 156

Transfer hens to an ovenproof pan and place in oven. Cook for about 12 minutes, until you can stick the leg and the juice runs clear. If the juice runs pink, cook for 3 minutes more.

Prepare brown stew sauce

In a saucepot over medium-high heat, melt butter and caramelize onions and garlic. Once caramelized, add tamarind paste and sugar, then stir. Add wine and bring to a boil, then cook at a simmer for 4 minutes.

Add tomatoes, planter's sauce, chicken stock, thyme and salt. Bring to a boil again and then cook at a fast simmer for 15 minutes.

Remove from heat and remove thyme sachet. Blend sauce in a blender, pulsing on low to let the steam out, and then on high until smooth.

Makes about 5 cups

A food processor will not work for blending this sauce, as it will not blend it smoothly enough. A good immersion hand blender will do the trick, though.

Assemble hens and sauce

When hens are done, remove from oven and place ½ hen on each of 4 plates. Spoon some sauce over each one. Garnish with scallions. Serve with Jamaican Rice and Peas (page 193) and a vegetable of your choice.

Jerk Pork Brine

3 tablespoons Jamaican
   Jerk Paste (page 145)
8 cups water
10 bay leaves
4 cinnamon sticks, bruised
24 allspice berries
20 cloves garlic, smashed with flat
   side of knife, skin on
4 Scotch bonnet chili peppers,
   poked with a knife
1¾ cups kosher salt
2 bunches fresh thyme
2 yellow onions,
   coarsely chopped, skin on
½ cup sugar
4 oranges, cut in half
4 limes, cut in half

In a large pot, bring all ingredients
to a boil. Continue to cook at a low
boil for about 10 minutes. Remove
from heat.

   Add 4 quarts ice to the hot brine
to help cool it quicker. When cooled
off, submerge pork in brine and
place in refrigerator for recommended time (12 to 24 hours). The longer
you brine, the more spice the pork
will have.
✽ I usually brine my pork for
recipes such as the "T-Bone" Pork
Chop in Bacardi Oakheart Guava
Sauce with Tropical Fruit Flambé
(page 202), where the sweetness in
the sauce balances all the spice in
the jerk.

Easy Jerk Chicken Marinade

½ cup olive oil
¼ cup teriyaki sauce
2 tablespoons Jerk Paste (page 145)
   or prepared Caribbean
   jerk paste or powder

Brines and Marinades

2 cloves fresh garlic, minced
½ cup minced yellow onion

In a stainless-steel bowl, whisk all
ingredients.
   Makes about 1 cup
✽ This is a great marinade for when
you don't have the time to do a traditional jerk paste or brine. I use it in
the Jerk Chicken Penne Pasta recipe
(page 170) and also substitute it for
marinating shrimp and vegetables,
simply because it's so fast and easy.

Mojo Marinade

2 tablespoons ground toasted cumin
2 tablespoons ground toasted
   coriander
5 cloves fresh garlic
4 scallions, white parts only
1 Scotch bonnet chili pepper, seeded
½ cup freshly squeezed orange juice

2 tablespoons freshly squeezed
   lime juice
½ cup olive oil

In a blender, purée all ingredients.
   Makes 2½ cups
✽ Mojo is considered a necessity in
Miami, where absolutely nobody of
Hispanic or Caribbean descent cooks
without it. It's like mirepoix to the
French: It begins a recipe and adds
another level of flavor at the same
time. You can use it as a marinade,
a dressing, a dip—it's terrific drizzled
over Crispy Fried Yucca or Twice-Fried
Yucca "Tostones" (page 183) or all of
the above. I also like to fool around
with the elements of the basic mojo
as sauces for recipes such as my
Berkshire Pork Tenderloin in Pomelo-
Coriander Mojo with Citrus-Braised
Onions (page 180).

Free-Range Chicken Pot Pie

We frequently roast chickens in our home. I usually buy organic free-range roasters. Because roasters are bigger, there are bound to be leftovers, but not quite enough to feed four people again. So by adding some nice vegetables, potatoes and herbs into a pie crust with the chicken leftovers, you can easily stretch them to make a solid meal. Making your own homemade crust is, of course, always appreciated, so I have provided a recipe. But in our household, it has become a stressful situation. My daughter, Ashley, and I have gotten into terrible wars over this one. We reached the point of actually hurling the dough across the kitchen in disapproval of each other's dough-making techniques. Have you ever been hit with dough? It's heavy, so it hurts—and it clearly becomes a case of too many cooks in the kitchen. This is just one reason why I don't disapprove of using store-bought pie crust.

MAKES ONE PIE

Chicken Pot Pie

4 tablespoons salted butter

1 cup onion, chopped

2 cloves garlic

¾ cup brunoised celery

¼ cup chopped fresh parsley

2 tablespoons chopped, freshly picked sage leaves

2 tablespoons fresh thyme leaves

3 tablespoons all-purpose flour

1½ cups chicken stock

2 carrots, diced, blanched in salted water

1 cup chopped broccoli, blanched in salted water

1 cup cauliflower, blanched in salted water

1 cup frozen baby peas (or fresh if you can find them)

1½ cups diced yellow potatoes, skin on

½ cup leftover chicken gravy
 (can substitute store-bought)

2–3 cups pulled free-range chicken meat
 (whatever you can pull from the bird)

Salt and pepper, to taste

Flaky Pie Crust

2 cups flour

1 teaspoon salt

2 sticks cold butter, cut into parts

⅓ cup cold water

continued on page 162

continued from page 160

Prepare chicken pot pie

In a stockpot, melt butter and sauté onion, garlic and celery until tender. Add parsley, sage and thyme. Stir in flour and add stock, carrots, broccoli, cauliflower, peas and potatoes. Cook for about 3 minutes, until sauce has thickened, and remove from heat.

Add chicken gravy and pulled chicken. Stir, season with salt and pepper, and reserve.

Prepare flaky pie crust

In a food processor, pulse flour, salt and a few pieces butter, periodically adding more pieces, until mixture is uniformly crumbly.

Add water all at once and pulse until mixture forms a ball. Do not overprocess or butter will begin to melt.

Remove dough ball from processor and divide in half. Press into discs and cover in plastic wrap. Refrigerate until ready to use.

Makes 1 top crust and 1 bottom crust

Prepare pie

Preheat oven to 375°F.

Using a rolling pin, flatten and carefully roll out the two pie-crust halves. Drape one into bottom of a 9-inch pie pan. Dock bottom crust with a fork.

Pour chicken-vegetable mixture into bottom crust. Cover with other rolled half of crust. Flute edges and cut 4 slits on top.

Bake for 40 to 45 minutes, until golden brown on top and steaming hot throughout center.

If you would like to use store-bought crust, Pillsbury is a great brand, and they also now make a gluten-free crust.

PANTRY

Papaya-Mango Salsa

2 cups brunoised firm, ripe papaya

2 cups brunoised firm, ripe mangoes

½ cup sugar
   (adjust per sweetness of mango)

Juice of 2–3 limes

¾ cup very finely chopped scallions,
   green only

½ teaspoon Scotch bonnet hot sauce

½ bunch cilantro, chopped

In a nonreactive stainless-steel bowl, combine all ingredients. Taste for sweetness and hot-sauce balance. Adjust accordingly.

   Makes about 4 cups

✳ This salsa requires no salt or pepper. It is supposed to be sweet to balance the high flavor and the zing of the spices in such dishes as the West Indian Curried Crab Cakes (page 60) and the Jamaican Jerk Paste-Marinated and Seared Bluefin Tuna (page 140). You can also get creative with it and mix it with the Roasted Garlic and Scotch Bonnet Aioli (page 109) to use as a condiment on a fried fish sandwich.

Black Bean Corn Salsa

½ cup brunoised red onion

2 tablespoons minced garlic

6 tablespoons garlic oil, divided
   (page 80)

2 cups corn, removed from cob

Kosher salt, to taste

½ cup small-diced red bell pepper

½ cup small-diced yellow bell pepper

1 teaspoon ground toasted cumin

1 tablespoon ground toasted
   coriander

2 cups black beans, cooked

¼ cup freshly squeezed lime juice

1 bunch cilantro, chopped

continued on page 164

Salsas and Chutneys

Salsas and chutneys are such refreshing, versatile condiments, I find new ways of using them all the time. I could easily put one into performance as a topper on tacos, or toss some in ceviche made with freshly caught fish or conch and eat it with crackers. I always find the sweetest tomatoes and onions available for preparing them, yet I also like mine spicy, which is why you see the addition of Scotch bonnet hot sauce in many of the recipes. I recommend doing as I do with the tomatoes and onions, but the sweaty brow is up to you.

continued from page 163

*1 bunch scallions, chopped fine,
green parts only*
Black pepper, to taste

In a small sauté pan over medium-high heat, sauté onions and garlic in 2 tablespoons garlic oil until tender. Remove from heat and scrape onto one end of a baking sheet. Set aside.

In a larger sauté pan over high heat, char corn in remaining garlic oil. Take care; corn will pop and fly out of the pan. Toss corn in pan as it chars and season with a little kosher salt. Turn off heat. Add corn to baking sheet next to onions. Return pan to stovetop but do not turn the heat back on. Drop in peppers and season with cumin and coriander. Toss mixture a few times, using only the residual heat in the pan and on the burner. Place peppers on remaining space on the baking sheet and place sheet in the refrigerator to cool.

When cool, combine in a bowl with beans, lime, cilantro, scallions, and salt and pepper, if necessary.

Makes 3½ to 4 cups

❋ This is a fantastic garnish for the Marinated Mahi-Mahi (page 112) but can also be served simply with chips as a starter.

Fire-Roasted Salsa Verde

1½ pounds tomatillos
12 serrano chili peppers
1 tablespoon olive oil
1 tablespoon kosher salt
½ cup minced sweet yellow onion
2 cloves garlic, minced
1 rounded teaspoon sugar
¾ cup chopped cilantro
3 tablespoons lime juice
Salt and pepper, to taste

Cut tomatillos in half. Cut serranos in half lengthwise and remove seeds. Rub peppers with olive oil, sprinkle with salt and place on a pan. Put pan under a broiler flame until tomatillos and peppers are slightly charred.

Place tomatillos and peppers in a food processor along with remaining ingredients and pulse until coarsely blended.

If more liquid is needed, add a little more lime juice and a bit of olive oil. Season to taste.

Makes 3 cups

❋ Pour over Queso Blanco-Stuffed Chicken Breast (page 176) or any other poultry or meat.

Pico de Gallo

*2 pounds tomatoes, firm, vine-ripe
beefsteak or plum, seeded*
½ cup brunoised Vidalia onions
1 large clove fresh garlic, minced
*½ cup thin-sliced green onion,
green parts only*
¾ cup chopped cilantro
*4–6 serrano peppers,
seeded and minced*
2 tablespoons kosher salt
1 teaspoon sugar
3 tablespoons olive oil
¼–½ cup freshly squeezed lime juice
*1 teaspoon Scotch bonnet hot sauce
(optional)*

Dice tomatoes as small as possible. Place in a nonreactive bowl.

Rinse garlic and onions in cold water and pat dry. Then add to tomatoes. Add remaining ingredients except lime juice and hot sauce, if using. Fold together with a spatula or a wooden spoon.

Add ¼ cup lime juice; mix and taste. If it needs more, add it. Do the same for hot sauce. The addition of more lime, hot sauce or salt is a personal decision. Some prefer it more acidic and spicy; others, less so.

* After salsa sits for a bit, the tomatoes will release liquid, so if you do not serve it right away, you will want to taste, perhaps drain and possibly reseason it. Use with the Marinated Mahi-Mahi in Breadfruit Taco Shells (page 112) or a recipe of your choice.

Sambal Pepper Sauce

½ cup olive oil

1 cup chopped fresh garlic

1 cup medium-diced yellow onion

12 red Thai chili peppers,
   stemmed and chopped

1½ pounds red Fresno chili peppers,
   stemmed and chopped

2 cups rice vinegar

2 tablespoons kosher salt

2 tablespoons light brown sugar

4 tablespoons fish sauce

1 tablespoon red pepper flakes
   (optional)

In a medium saucepan over medium-high heat, place oil. Add garlic and onion and sweat them. Then add peppers and sauté for 2 minutes. Add remaining ingredients, stir and remove from heat.

Place in a food processor and pulse a few times until it reaches the consistency of salsa. Taste; if you desire more heat, add red pepper flakes.

Chill and store in glass Mason jars. Keeps for up to 2 months.

Makes about 3 cups

* It is wise to wear gloves while preparing any hot-pepper sauce. Also, while handling chili peppers, you should keep your hands away from your eyes. Use the sauce in Cumin- and Coriander-Dusted Mahi-Mahi (page 128) or a recipe of your choice.

Mango-Cherry-Chili Chutney

4 tablespoons Herb Butter
   (page 27)

2 cups diced red onion

½ cup thin-sliced garlic

4 cups medium-diced mango

2 chipotle peppers in adobo sauce,
   chopped with the sauce,
   which will stick to the peppers

¼ cup tomato paste

1½ cups white wine

⅓ cup apple cider vinegar

2 cups minced Amarena cherries

2 tablespoons ground coriander

2 tablespoons curry powder

2 tablespoons kosher salt

1 bunch cilantro, chopped

In a skillet, melt butter and sauté onion and garlic until tender, 4 or 5 minutes. Add mango and the chipotle, then mix in tomato paste and stir for about 2 minutes.

Add wine, then all remaining ingredients except cilantro. Simmer over low heat for 30 to 40 minutes.

Meanwhile, prepare an ice bath.

If chutney becomes too dry, you may need to add ½ to 1 cup water and reduce further. Mix and taste for balanced flavors of sweetness, acidity, spice and saltiness. When satisfied with the flavor, remove from heat and chill in the ice bath.

After chutney has cooled, add cilantro. Use or refrigerate for future use. It keeps for several months in an airtight container in the refrigerator.

Makes 4½ cups

* This chutney is awesome on top of the 50/50 Bombay Burgers (page 102) or in the Pan-Roasted Duck sauce (page 174). It's also delicious when eaten as a garnish with curry dishes, such as in the Grandma Iris Country Curried Chicken (page 166).

Grandma Iris Country Curried Chicken

with White Potatoes, Carrots, Chayote, Ginger and Fresh Coconut Milk

Iris Day, my Chinese Jamaican pseudo-mom, alias "Dragon Lady," taught me how to make curried chicken 32 years ago. She made the best! Her daughter Rosalie and I would watch her with a cigarette hanging out of her mouth, Scotch in a Baccarat crystal glass in one hand and the other stirring a wooden spoon. That cigarette ash would get longer and longer and just as we thought it was going to break off into the curry pot, she would simply turn her head and the ash would drop to the floor. We would laugh so hard, but she was oblivious as to why. So in the end, it wasn't Rothmans ash (or Scotch) that made her curry special, but the blend of seasonings and the love that she put into it. I do mine the same way, with just a couple of minor differences: minus the cigarette and replacing the Scotch with a glass of wine. But the wooden spoon, the spices and the love for the dish are all just like hers, and I don't allow a single drop of anything to fall on the floor.

SERVES SIX TO EIGHT

1 (3½-pound) whole chicken
5 tablespoons kosher salt, divided
2 fresh limes, cut into quarters
4 tablespoons cumin seeds
4 tablespoons coriander seeds
2 tablespoons allspice berries
6 tablespoons Madras curry powder
4 tablespoons vegetable oil
6 cloves fresh garlic, smashed and chopped
2 cups diced yellow onion
3 cups chicken stock
1 cup diced carrots

1 bunch fresh thyme, tied with butcher's twine
1½ cups diced vine-ripe tomatoes,
    as many seeds removed as possible
1 cinnamon stick
Juice from 1½-inch-long fresh ginger root
1 cup fresh coconut milk (page 168),
    or 1 can coconut milk
1 whole Scotch bonnet chili pepper
1½ cups diced potatoes, washed and skin left on
2 cups large-diced chayote, washed and skin left on

continued on page 168

continued from page 166

In a clean sink, cut chicken down the breast bone and split open. Rinse with a little cold water. Remove any excess fat pockets and hanging skin. (I sometimes remove the skin altogether if I want it to be a little healthier. But while the skin does add fat, it also adds flavor.)

Place chicken on a large cutting board and pat dry. Sprinkle with 3 tablespoons salt and rub all over, inside and out, with cut limes. Pat dry.

Using a cleaver, break chicken into sections. I like cutting the thighs and breasts in half, giving you 4 segments of each. Set cut chicken aside on a platter.

In a small skillet, toast cumin, coriander and allspice over medium-high heat. Shake continuously so spices don't scorch. As they begin to pop and become aromatic, remove from heat, then place in a spice grinder and pulverize. Combine with Madras curry and rub half the mixture all over chicken. Reserve the other half.

Set a Dutch oven large enough to hold chicken over medium-high flame. Heat oil, then add chicken pieces a few at a time, meat side down, and brown on one side. After each piece browns, remove and return to platter. (Don't worry about contaminating chicken with raw juice, because you'll be cooking it again.)

Use the same oil and chicken renderings to sauté garlic and onion. Once onions are al dente, add reserved spices and stir. Then add chicken stock and stir again.

Reintroduce chicken and add carrots, thyme, tomatoes, cinnamon stick, ginger juice, coconut milk and remaining salt. Float Scotch bonnet in the pot. Bring to a boil, then reduce to a simmer, cover and cook for about 20 minutes.

Uncover, add potatoes and chayote, and simmer, uncovered, for 30 minutes more. The sauce should thicken some. Taste for seasoning. Remove Scotch bonnet, chop and return it to curry for extra spiciness.

Serve in bowls immediately, or allow to cool, refrigerate and reheat when ready to eat. This is one of those dishes that get better after a little time, allowing the flavors to soak in.

❋ The curry is excellent served with steamed white rice, and some of the Mango-Cherry-Chili Chutney goes well with it too. Squeezing fresh ginger juice is easy. Just wash a nob of ginger and grate it, skin and all, using a microplane. Then, wearing kitchen gloves or using clean hands, pick up the shavings and squeeze out all the juices into a container. Discard the fibrous shavings, leaving just the fresh juice.

How to Make Fresh Coconut Milk

It's very easy to buy canned coconut milk (though some brands taste better than others, of course). But if you have a little patience, a large nail, a hammer and a strong blender, you can make the best-tasting coconut milk, which in turn makes some of the best-tasting recipes.

Ingredients
1 (or more) coconut
4 cups water

Supplies
Big roofing nail
Hammer
Fine mesh strainer
Butter knife
Cheesecloth

Select good coconuts
To identify a good coconut, pick one up and shake it. Listen to hear if there is sufficient liquid. If you don't hear a lot of liquid, odds are that coconut is old. Next, look at the three dark circles (or eyes) at one end of the coconut. If they have any mildew or smell of mildew, they are old and you should choose another.

Prepare coconut milk
In a large pot on the stove, set the water to boil.

Prepare a bowl covered with a fine mesh strainer. Set aside. Take the long nail and hold the coconut firmly on end. With the hammer, tap the nail and pop a hole all the way through the first eye into the coconut. Repeat with the other eyes. Tip the coconut over your prepared bowl and let the coconut water drain through the strainer into the bowl. Repeat with the others if you choose to do more than one coconut. Reserve the coconut water after straining through cheesecloth. Set aside. (Note: Coconut water is very high in potassium and very good for rehydrating, especially after a long night out—just saying.)

Prepare coconut meat

Take the drained coconut in your hand and, on a hard surface, hold it firmly, with the eye end parallel to the surface. With the hammer, begin hitting the coconut firmly around the middle, turning it as you do. At some point, the shell will begin to crack. Continue hitting and turning until it cracks completely in half.

Using a strong butter knife, begin prying the coconut meat from the inner shell; it will pop out in pieces. Once all the meat has been extracted, discard the shell and cut the meat in 2-inch pieces. Place in a heat-resistant bowl.

Remove the boiling water from the stove and pour over the coconut pieces in the bowl. Allow to sit for 25 minutes.

Set up another bowl with a cheesecloth over it.

In 2-cup batches in a blender, purée coconut and water on high speed until the mixture is smooth. Pour into the cheesecloth and wring the liquid out into the bowl. Unwrap the cheesecloth and discard the coconut trash. Repeat until all the coconut is strained.

You now have a rich, homemade coconut milk to use in recipes. It will keep for up to 2 days in the refrigerator but is generally very perishable, so don't keep it any longer than that. It also freezes well. I recommend making more than you need and freezing extra for the next time you wish to cook.

Jerk Chicken Penne Pasta

I created this recipe in my early days as a chef at Norma's on the Beach on Lincoln Road. It was effortless and versatile. I was inexperienced, and this was a basic recipe where I could change out the protein and offer it up as a different dish. Sometimes it would have jerk veal; other times, jerk shrimp. Occasionally, I made it vegetarian and would even offer jerk tofu or just jerk vegetables. Customers seemed to love it no matter which version was presented.

SERVES SIX

1 recipe Easy Jerk Chicken Marinade (page 159)
3 tablespoons salted butter
2 pounds boneless chicken breasts, julienned
¾ cup shiitake mushrooms, julienned
½ cup sun-dried tomatoes
2 cups heavy cream
1 teaspoon chicken bouillon (see note)
1 bunch scallions, chopped
¼ cup fresh basil, chiffonaded
1 pound penne pasta,
    cooked according to directions on package
Salt and pepper, to taste

Cover chicken with marinade and let stand for at least 1 hour or refrigerate overnight.

Once chicken has cured sufficiently, pour off excess marinade. In a large skillet, melt butter and sauté chicken over medium-high heat until cooked halfway through. Add mushrooms, tomatoes, cream and bouillon.

Sauté for about 3 minutes, until cream has thickened. Add pasta, salt and pepper to sauce and mix well. Taste and adjust seasonings. Finish with scallions and basil, toss again, remove from heat and serve immediately.

❋ I prefer to use Better Than Bouillon Chicken Base because it has no MSG. You may decide not to use any salt whatsoever in the sauce and use only the chicken bouillon. As always, that's up to you.

Leftover Turkey Shepherd's Pie

with Buttery Potato Purée and Old Quebec Vintage Cheddar

Like everyone else, I've become tired of using yesterday's bird as tomorrow's soup. I needed to find another way to use up the second-day turkey. After all, turkey soup is great, but sometimes the poultry can become stringy. Since a Thanksgiving-type meal usually involves not just a big bird but leftover potatoes and veggies as well, I figured it would be terrific to combine them all in one new dish. And it is, especially when preceded by a crisp green salad and partnered with a nice dry rosé.

MAKES SIX 6-OUNCE RAMEKINS OR EIGHT 4-OUNCE RAMEKINS

4 tablespoons butter

1 cup diced onions

1 cup diced carrots

½ cup diced celery

4 tablespoons all-purpose flour

2 tablespoons tomato paste

½ cup dry white wine

3 cups chicken or turkey stock

1 tablespoon Worcestershire sauce

1½–2 pounds leftover turkey meat, diced

½ cup diced turnips, boiled in salted water
   for 5–10 minutes, until tender

¾ cup frozen peas, defrosted

½ cup shaved Brussels sprouts, blanched
   in salted water for 2 minutes and plunged
   into ice bath to retain color, then strained

4 cups leftover mashed potatoes,
   puréed with extra butter

1 cup grated Old Quebec Vintage Cheddar

Preheat oven to 375°F.

In a skillet, melt butter over medium-high heat. Sauté onions and carrots until tender. Add flour and mix into a roux.

Add tomato paste and stir. Add wine, stock and Worcestershire sauce. Bring to a simmer while whisking out the lumps. It should simmer until thickened.

Mix in turkey, turnips, peas and Brussels sprouts. Stir until well-mixed; taste for seasoning.

Fill a 4- or 6-ounce ramekin with turkey mixture, leaving ½ inch of room from top. Fill remaining space with puréed potatoes and sprinkle with grated cheddar. Repeat with remaining ramekins.

Bake in oven until potatoes are golden brown.

✳ **Remember: This is a leftover turkey shepherd's pie, so any leftover vegetables may be substituted into this recipe. You are not limited to the vegetables listed.**

Pan-Roasted Duck Breast

with Mango-Cherry-Chili Chutney Sauce

Duck is one of my favorite birds. My son Christian is a hunter and gatherer of many different animals, amphibians, crustaceans and fish. I always know that as each hunting season opens, I will wake up to find those "things"—lobsters, gators, frogs, redfish, snook and, yes, plenty of duck—in my coolers. When I talk about respecting the animals you kill, he's a guy who does just that, and allows me to do the same. Indeed, my "redneck" son has inspired many a recipe by providing me with freshly harvested, in-season, locally sourced ingredients.

SERVES SIX

¾ cup Mango-Cherry-Chili Chutney (page 165)
6 (8-ounce) boneless duck breasts
Salt and pepper, to taste
4 tablespoons Clarified Butter (page 27)
¼ cup Grand Marnier
Juice of 3 sweet Florida oranges (no seeds)
2 tablespoons sherry vinegar
3 tablespoons store-bought poultry glace
Chopped cilantro, for garnish

Preheat oven to 400°F.

Using a sharp knife, make slits in skin of duck. Season with salt and pepper on both sides.

Melt butter in a sauté pan over medium-high and render duck breasts, skin side down, for 8 to 10 minutes. Lower heat if skin is getting too dark. Once skin is a nice golden brown, turn breasts over and cook for 1 to 2 minutes more.

Pour off fat and reserve, then place duck on a baking sheet. Place in oven and cook for 5 to 10 minutes, until breast is medium-rare. Remove from oven and let rest.

Meanwhile, in the sauté pan the duck was cooked in, set over medium-high heat, pour in Grand Marnier to deglaze pan. Add orange juice and vinegar and simmer for about 3 minutes. Add poultry glace and chutney and simmer until sauce becomes syrupy. Reduce heat to the lowest setting and keep sauce warm.

Place duck on a cutting board and slice on the bias. Divide among 6 plates and spoon warmed chutney sauce over duck breasts. Garnish with cilantro and serve immediately.

Queso Blanco-Stuffed Chicken Breasts

with Fire-Roasted Salsa Verde

Mexican flavors always seem so fresh and light, but let the truth be told: I guess they're not always so much on the "light" side. That said, this recipe is anything but heavy, and it is certainly vibrant. Indeed, it's a delight even on the hottest summer night when your appetite seems to have waned with the breeze. The flavors in here will definitely make you find your hunger again.

SERVES EIGHT

1 recipe Fire-Roasted Salsa Verde (page 164)
4–6 tablespoons Clarified Butter (page 27)
2 large yellow bell peppers
2 large red bell peppers
2 teaspoons salted butter
1 pound baby spinach
Kosher salt and black pepper, to taste
8 ounces cream cheese, at room temperature
2 ounces queso blanco, at room temperature
2 ounces feta cheese, at room temperature
¾ cup scallions, chopped
8 skinless, boneless chicken breasts, pounded thin
8 leaves culantro (can substitute cilantro leaves)

Preheat oven to 400°F.

Prepare salsa and butter.

Place bell peppers on a baking sheet. Roast peppers until parts of the skin are golden brown. Remove and place in a stainless-steel bowl and cover with plastic wrap. Set aside for 15 minutes.

Reduce oven heat to 350°F.

In a skillet, sauté spinach in salted butter and sprinkle with salt and pepper. Remove from skillet and drain and cool on paper towels.

In a bowl, mix cheeses with scallions. Set aside.

Peel and seed the roasted peppers and julienne into strips. Set aside.

Place pounded chicken breasts on large piece of plastic wrap on a cutting board or countertop. Sprinkle breasts with salt and pepper and begin layering each breast with cheese mixture, spinach, peppers and culantro. Roll each chicken breast tightly, like a cigar, and tie in three places with butcher's twine.

In a large skillet, sear each chicken breast on all sides in clarified butter and then place on a baking sheet. Finish cooking in the oven until done, 10 to 15 minutes. Remove from the oven. Let rest for 5 minutes and then cut the butcher's twine. Slice on the bias.

Place stuffed breasts on a platter for service and pour salsa verde over them. Serve with Jamaican Rice and Peas (page 193).

CHAPTER 7

MEATS

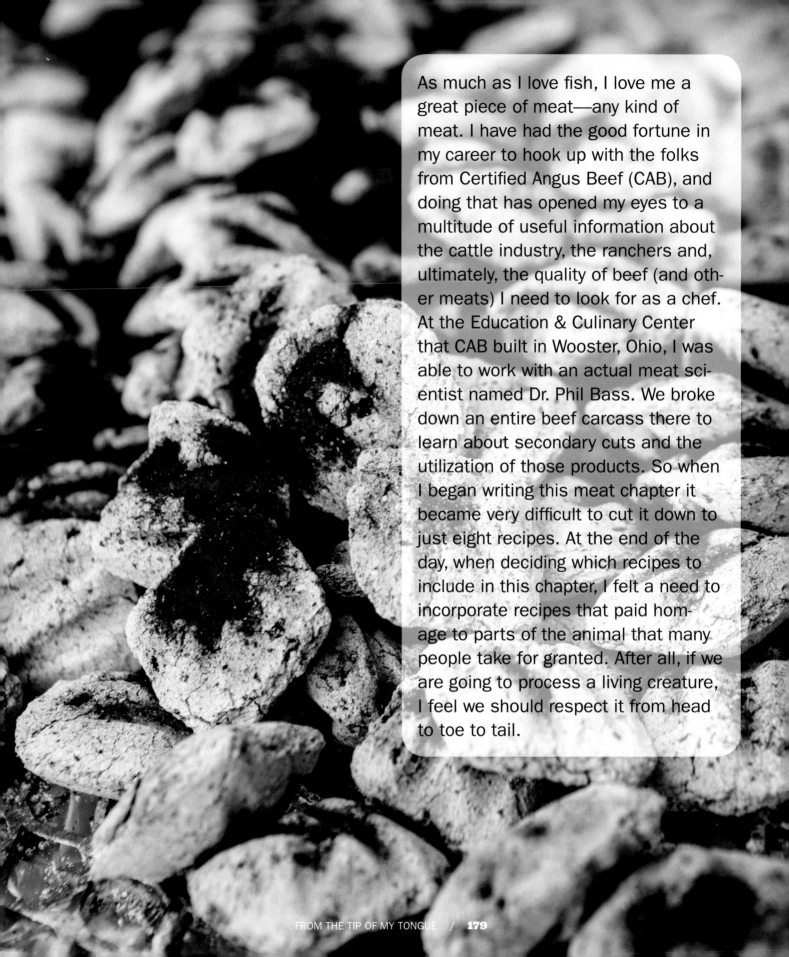

As much as I love fish, I love me a great piece of meat—any kind of meat. I have had the good fortune in my career to hook up with the folks from Certified Angus Beef (CAB), and doing that has opened my eyes to a multitude of useful information about the cattle industry, the ranchers and, ultimately, the quality of beef (and other meats) I need to look for as a chef. At the Education & Culinary Center that CAB built in Wooster, Ohio, I was able to work with an actual meat scientist named Dr. Phil Bass. We broke down an entire beef carcass there to learn about secondary cuts and the utilization of those products. So when I began writing this meat chapter it became very difficult to cut it down to just eight recipes. At the end of the day, when deciding which recipes to include in this chapter, I felt a need to incorporate recipes that paid homage to parts of the animal that many people take for granted. After all, if we are going to process a living creature, I feel we should respect it from head to toe to tail.

Berkshire Pork Tenderloins in Pomelo-Coriander Mojo
with Citrus-Braised Onions

Sometime in the 1950s, people started thinking pork needed to be leaner, less fatty. So they convinced the pork producers to starve the little piggies and change their diets to make them skinny. And then they said it had to be cooked well-done! What kind of nonsense was that? So several years back, we chefs started saying we needed a fatter pig that could be cooked to a nice, juicy medium-rare. Doesn't that make sense? That's when the pork producers introduced those of us who work behind the scenes to free-roaming Berkshire hogs, gorging themselves on oats, barley and wheat. Those small grains created wonderful marbling and darker meat in the breed. The pork is more expensive, but the flavor is so good it's clearly worth the spiked price. When you prepare this breed of pork, you can really taste the difference.

SERVES FOUR

Tenderloins

2 pounds Berkshire pork tenderloins

¼ cup olive oil

2 tablespoons ground coriander

1 tablespoon ground cumin

1 tablespoon kosher salt

4–6 tablespoons Clarified Butter (page 27)

1 recipe Citrus-Zested Braised Onions (page 183)

1 recipe Crispy Fried Yucca (page 183)

Pomelo-Coriander Mojo

½ cup olive oil

8 cloves garlic, chopped

1½ cups sliced sweet yellow onion

1–2 tablespoons red pepper flakes

½ cup freshly squeezed orange juice

1 cup freshly squeezed pomelo juice (can substitute ruby red grapefruit juice)

¼ cup freshly squeezed lime juice

2 tablespoons sherry vinegar

½ cup Bacardi Oakheart rum

continued on page 182

continued from page 180

¾ cup orange marmalade

1 cup pomelo segments, membranes removed

½ cup agave nectar

1 tablespoon ground coriander

2 tablespoons kosher salt, or to taste

¼ cup chopped parsley

¼ cup chopped cilantro

Prepare pork tenderloins

Preheat oven to 400° F. Make sure the rack is in the middle of the oven.

With a sharp knife, clean off any silver skin from tenderloins. Rub them with olive oil and season with spices and salt. Set aside and let come to room temperature.

Heat a large sauté pan over high heat and melt butter. Add pork tenderloins, being careful not to splatter. Brown all sides of tenderloins, then transfer pan to oven and cook until internal temperature reaches 135°F. Remove and let rest before slicing. Temperature will rise about 5 degrees, or to medium-rare, by the time you are done preparing the onions and fried yucca.

Prepare mojo

Prepare an ice bath.

In a skillet, heat olive oil and sauté onions and garlic. When just tender, add red pepper flakes and sauté. Add citrus juices, vinegar, rum, marmalade and pomelo segments and simmer for 4 minutes.

Add agave nectar, stir and remove from heat. Pour into a stainless-steel bain marie and place in the ice bath. Once cooled, ladle half the mojo into a blender and blend on medium speed until smooth. Then return to the unblended sauce and whisk in remaining ingredients.

Makes 2½ to 3 cups

Plate tenderloins

After pork has rested, slice tenderloins thinly on the bias. Place some fried yucca on each of 4 plates and fan pork on top. Then spoon mojo on top of pork, and finish by topping with the onions.

Citrus-Zested Braised Onions

½ cup olive oil
20 cloves garlic, slivered
6 onions, julienned along the ribs
¼ cup freshly squeezed orange juice
¼ cup freshly squeezed lime juice
2 tablespoons oregano
1 tablespoon coriander, ground
1 teaspoon cumin, ground
1 tablespoon sugar
1 tablespoon kosher salt
1 teaspoon red pepper flakes

In a skillet, heat oil, then sweat garlic and onions. Add juices, oregano, coriander, cumin, sugar, salt and red pepper flakes. Stir and simmer for 1 minute. Remove from heat. Allow to cool and use as a garnish.
✳ These onions are an essential part of the Mojo-Roasted Pulled Pork with Citrus-Zested Braised Onions in a Twice-Fried Yucca "Tostones" Sandwich (page 116) and also go well with the Berkshire Pork Tenderloins in Pomelo-Coriander Mojo (page 180).

Crispy Fried Yucca

1 bag frozen yucca
2 tablespoons garlic powder
Vegetable oil, for frying
Kosher salt, to taste

Cook yucca according to package directions by boiling in salted water and 2 tablespoons garlic powder. Cook until soft. Drain and cool. When cooled, cut into fries and remove fibers.

Prepare a FryDaddy or a deep skillet with oil for frying and allow it to reach the proper temperature. Fry cooked yucca in batches until crisp, then remove with a slotted spoon and place on paper towels to drain. Salt to taste.

Onions and Yucca

✳ Frozen yucca is found in most grocery stores. It's an excellent starch alternative to regular old white potatoes and can substitute for them whenever they are called for— mashed, steamed, fried and so forth.

Twice-Fried Yucca "Tostones"

4 pieces salted, boiled yucca,
*   about 4 inches long*
*   and 1½ inches thick*
2 cups vegetable oil
Salt and pepper, to taste

In a deep skillet or FryDaddy, heat oil to 300°F.

Make sure the core of the yucca has been removed from the center of the tubers. Place all 4 pieces, one by one, into the hot oil. When yucca becomes golden brown, remove with a slotted spoon and place on paper towels to blot off the oil.

Using a kitchen mallet, smash each yucca into a flat (about ¼-inch-thick) rectangular slab. It will not be a perfect rectangle, but try to get all slabs uniform in size. Now drop them in the hot oil for a second fry, until they become just a bit more golden brown. Remove from oil, blot on paper towels and season with salt and pepper.
✳ Use these in place of bread for sandwiches, as in the Mojo-Roasted Pulled Pork with Citrus-Zested Braised Onions in a Twice-Fried Yucca "Tostones" Sandwich (page 116), or as the base for meats or fish in main-course servings.

Braised Oxtail Ravioli

with Brandied Mushroom Ragù, Charred Corn
and Micro Arugula

You can prepare so many great dishes with oxtail. The stock alone is deliciously rich in and of itself, and it is awesome done simply as a hearty winter soup. But here I use one of my favorite methods: reducing it down to a fine demi-glace. You may think it is difficult, with prepping and of course stuffing the ravioli, but it is so worth it. I have made it easier for you by cheating and letting you use gyoza skins, which work perfectly fine as ravioli dough. But if you want to roll out some ravioli dough, by all means, don't let me stop you.

SERVES SIX

Braised Oxtail

8 cloves garlic, chopped

¼ cup soy sauce

¼ cup whole-grain mustard

½ cup tomato paste

2 rosemary sprigs, leaves pulled off

¼ cup sherry vinegar

½ cup canola oil

Kosher salt and freshly ground black pepper, to taste

6 pounds oxtail, cut 2½ inches and trimmed

½ cup all-purpose flour

10 shallots, chopped

1 large onion, chopped

2 carrots, chopped

2 stalks celery, chopped

4 bay leaves

1 whole bunch thyme, twisted

1 bottle port wine (an inexpensive ruby is good)

Oxtail Ravioli

4 tablespoons salted butter

1 cup brunoised yellow onion

½ cup brunoised carrots

½ cup brunoised celery

1 tablespoon ground cumin

1 tablespoon ground coriander

1 teaspoon paprika

¼ cup chopped celery leaves

2 cloves garlic, smashed and chopped

2 egg yolks

¼ cup Dijon mustard

½ cup grated Manchego cheese

½ cup grated Parmesan cheese

8 ounces Mascarpone cheese

1 teaspoon seeded and minced
   Scotch bonnet chili pepper (optional)

¼ teaspoon freshly ground black pepper

2 rounded teaspoons kosher salt

1 cup braised, shredded oxtail meat, picked off bones

3 packs round gyoza skins

1 whole egg, for egg wash

continued on page 186

continued from page 185

Brandied Mushroom Ragù

4 tablespoons salted butter

1 cup halved chanterelle mushrooms
(can substitute button mushrooms)

2 ears corn, kernels cut off cob

½ cup sliced scallions, green parts only

½ cup brandy

1 cup braised, shredded oxtail meat, picked off bones

8 ounces micro arugula

Prepare braised oxtail

Preheat oven to 400°F.

In a food processor, place garlic, soy sauce, mustard, ¼ cup tomato paste, rosemary, sherry, ½ cup canola oil, and salt and pepper and pulse for 2 minutes.

In a stainless steel bowl, place oxtail and coat each piece with the garlic-soy mixture. Marinate for at least 2 hours, preferably overnight, in the refrigerator.

After marinating oxtail, shake off excess marinade back into bowl. Reserve for braising liquid.

Place flour in a clean bowl. Sprinkle a little salt and pepper on oxtail pieces and then dust them piece by piece in flour, shaking off any excess. Place oxtail on a baking sheet and brown in oven for about 15 minutes.

Once oxtail is browned, set aside in a bowl. Transfer about 4 tablespoons cooking oils and any unburned tasty bits from tray into a Dutch oven. Discard excess oil.

Lower oven to 350°F.

Place Dutch oven on stove and heat to medium-high. Add shallots, onion, carrots, celery, bay leaves and thyme. Sauté just until vegetables are tender.

Add remaining tomato paste, stir, and add port, stock and reserved marinade. Add oxtail. If liquid doesn't cover the meat completely, add some water. Stir again, bringing to a boil on the stovetop. Turn off heat and remove from stove.

Cover pan and cook in oven for about 2¾ hours, until meat strips off easily from the bones.

When done, let oxtail cool until it can easily be handled. Strip off meat, discarding fat and bones, and reserve the meat for the raviolis. Strain and reserve the stock for sauce. After oxtail stock has been refrigerated overnight, a fat cap will form. Peel it off and throw it away. Your stock is now ready to be reduced to a demi-glace.

Makes about 5 quarts oxtail and sauce

❋ **This recipe makes much more than necessary for preparing ravioli. You can make more ravioli than you need and keep them in food-saver bags in the freezer; freeze the oxtail and sauce for reheating over pasta; or use as the filling in killer grilled-cheese sandwiches another day.**

Prepare oxtail ravioli

Remove eggs, mustard and cheeses from refrigerator and allow to come to room temperature. Move on to next steps as they come up to temperature.

In a large skillet over medium-high heat, melt butter and sauté onion, carrot and celery until tender, 4 or 5 minutes. Add cumin, coriander, paprika, celery leaves and chopped garlic, turn down heat to low and cook for 5 minutes. Remove from heat, scrape into a large stainless-steel bowl and set aside to cool.

In a food processor, place room-temperature egg yolks, mustard, cheeses, Scotch bonnet, and salt and pepper. Pulse until mixed. Add cooled vegetable mixture and blend until smooth.

Scrape into a big stainless-steel bowl and add shredded oxtail. Put on gloves and hand-mix well.

With the remaining whole egg, make an egg wash. Stuff each gyoza skin with about 2 tablespoons oxtail mixture. Place the oxtail mix in the center of the gyoza skin. Brush the edges with the egg wash and place another skin on top. Carefully work your fingers from center to the edges, pressing out any air bubbles and sealing the ravioli. As an added measure to keep them sealed, crimp with fork tines. Then place all of the raviolis on a sheet tray and freeze before use. (Freezing the raviolis before boiling produces a better final product.)

❋ This recipe is easy to make well ahead of time. Double the recipe and make extra for future use. They will keep up to 3 months if frozen in a proper food-saver vacuum storage bag.

Prepare brandied mushroom ragù

Transfer reserved oxtail stock to a pot over high heat and bring to a boil. Lower heat and cook at a low boil, reducing stock until syrupy, about 45 to 60 minutes. Taste for seasoning and adjust as needed.

In a sauté pan, melt butter over medium heat and sauté mushrooms. As they begin to color, add corn and sauté for about 2 minutes. Add brandy and cook off the alcohol, 2 minutes more. Add oxtail meat and sauté for 3 minutes. Add scallions, then remove from heat and set aside, until all the raviolis have been cooked.

Plate ravioli and ragù

Prepare a large pot of salted water and set to boil. Drop ravioli in. I suggest about 4 to 6 per person for a main-course serving, as they are very rich. When they begin to float, remove with a slotted spoon and divide among 4 curved plates or bowls. Drizzle with ragu, making sure to divvy mushrooms and corn, and top with micro arugula.

Certified Angus Beef Grilled Flat Iron Steak

with Local Mango Chimichurri

The flat iron steak used to be thought of as a tough piece of meat. It took a meat scientist—yes, a meat scientist—to figure out how to butcher the shoulder properly, leaving the thick connective tissue behind. The result was a deliciously juicy, tender and flavorful steak that takes well to a grill or pan-searing. Just a bit of salt and pepper, and some of my Local Mango Chimichurri, are all this steak requires to work beautifully.

SERVES SIX

6 (8-ounce) Certified Angus Beef flat iron steaks
¼ cup olive oil
Smoked sea salt
Freshly ground black pepper
1 recipe Local Mango Chimichurri (page 51)

Rub steaks with olive oil. Season and set aside.
Prepare chimichurri and set aside.
Prepare your grill. Once heated to about 425°F, cook steaks to your preferred temperature.
Serve with Local Mango Chimichurri.

Several shops online offer different flavors of sea salt. I purchase my smoked sea salt, a variety called Fumée de Sel, from the Artisan Salt Company. You can get yours there or from whoever else carries good-quality salts that are flavored naturally.

Curry-Braised Lamb Necks

with Potato, Cannellini Beans, Caribbean Pumpkin, Carrots and Chayote

I was on a kick of utilizing meats, sometimes called secondary cuts of animals, that people rarely think about eating. Maybe it's because they don't know how, or it could be that they think the local grocer doesn't sell them. But after spending some time with the folks at Certified Angus Beef and really learning about these parts, I began applying my knowledge to most of the animals I cooked. I inquired from my meat purveyor about lamb necks. I asked him to cut them horizontally, about 1¼ inches thick, so that they would resemble the shape and heft of osso buco. I learned quickly, as my father had with beef tongue, not to tell the kids what they were eating so that they would simply dig in and love it. So when my children asked, "What's for dinner, Mom?" my standard reply was "Lamb osso buco." I don't know, it just sounded nicer. But I'll tell you one thing— they certainly know what they're eating now, and they still savor it.

SERVES FOUR

6 tablespoons Madras curry powder, divided

Kosher salt and freshly cracked black pepper, to taste

3–4 pounds lamb necks
 (about 4 necks, cut horizontally
 into 1½-inch pieces)

¼ cup olive oil

2 cups diced yellow onion

6 cloves garlic, chopped

1 cup small-diced carrots

3 celery stalks, sliced thin

¼ cup chopped celery leaves

1 bunch thyme, leaves picked, stems discarded

¼ cup tomato paste

1 tablespoon ground cumin powder

½ teaspoon ground cinnamon

1 teaspoon smoked paprika

3 tablespoons kosher salt

¼ cup vinegar

2 cups red table wine

2 cups diced vine-ripe tomatoes

1 cup small-diced chayote

2 quarts beef stock

1½ cups medium-diced Yukon potatoes

1½ cups cooked cannellini beans

continued on page 192

continued from page 190

Preheat oven to 400°F, making sure the baking rack is in the middle.

In a small bowl, mix 4 tablespoons Madras curry powder with salt and pepper. Place lamb necks on a half sheet pan and season with mixture on all sides. Roast in oven for 15 to 20 minutes, until slightly browned.

Meanwhile, in a 6½-quart Dutch oven or roasting pan large enough to hold the necks, vegetables and stock, place olive oil. Add onion, garlic, carrots, celery stalks and leaves, and thyme and sauté for 4 to 5 minutes over medium-high heat. Add tomato paste, cumin, cinnamon, paprika, remaining curry powder, salt, vinegar and wine, and cook, stirring, for about 4 minutes.

Add lamb necks, scraping all the juicy bits from the baking sheet into the Dutch oven. Add the tomatoes, chayote and beef stock. Lower oven to 350°F.

If the necks are not covered, add a bit more beef stock, then bring lamb to a simmer. Cover pan and transfer to oven. Cook for another 2 hours or until the meat around the neck bone is tender and pulls away easily. After the first 1½ hours of braising, uncover pan and add potatoes. Once lamb necks are fork-tender, add cooked beans and taste for seasoning, adding more salt and pepper if needed. Skim off any fat that has risen to the top with a ladle. Serve over steamed basmati rice if desired.

Lamb necks are rich and flavorful. I always cook a little extra than I need and use it for sandwiches with goat cheese and cucumber slices for lunch for the kitchen crew the next day. Don't see them in the grocery store? Ask the clerks at the butcher department. They're usually kept in the back for those special requests.

Sides

I like to pair a specific starch or vegetable with each dish we serve in the restaurants. Here, I offer instead several of each that can go with a multitude of proteins. They're a bit different from what you might think of as the norm—like the Fig-Walnut Potato Gratin, for instance, or the Parmesan Oven-Roasted Spaghetti Squash—but they're a big hit with everyone who tries them.

Jamaican Rice and Peas

There are as many versions of rice and peas throughout the Caribbean as there are islands. In fact, each specific island has its own way of making this dish, and although a lot of them are named rice and peas or something similar, at times the ingredients can vary greatly. My favorite version of Jamaican rice and peas is the one cooked with what they call

gungo peas, or what Puerto Ricans call gandules. In the United States, we know them as pigeon peas. When I really want to knock people out with authenticity, I make fresh coconut milk, but in this recipe I use canned. I do give the recipe for fresh coconut milk (page 168); one day, try making this recipe with that. There is a flavor differential, but there's also a lot more time involved.

¾ cup small-diced onion
2 large cloves fresh garlic, minced
4 tablespoons Herb Butter (page 27)
8 allspice berries
2 tablespoons kosher salt
1 Scotch bonnet chili pepper, whole
1 bunch fresh thyme, tied with
butcher's twine
1 bunch scallions,
    tied with butcher's twine
2¼ cups water
1 can coconut milk
2 cups Mahatma rice
1 can pigeon peas
    (I recommend Goya brand)

In a 6-quart pot with a tight-fitting lid, sauté onion and garlic in butter over medium heat. Add allspice, salt, Scotch bonnet, thyme and scallions and stir gently.

Add water and coconut milk and bring to a boil. Once it reaches a rolling boil, add rice and peas and stir once or twice. Turn heat to low, cover and cook for 15 minutes.

Uncover and turn off heat. Using a spatula or wooden spoon, give it one good stir, re-cover pot and let rest for 20 minutes more before serving. Remove thyme, scallions and the whole Scotch bonnet. If you like a lot of

continued on page 194

continued from page 193

heat, cut up Scotch bonnet, remove seeds and stir back into the mixture.

Serve immediately.

Serves 6

Caribbean Mac 'n' Cheese

My ex-mother-in-law, Dorit Hutson, was an amazing cook. There were several Caribbean dishes she taught me while I was married to her son Charles, and this was one of them. She never used flour or béchamel to thicken her mac 'n' cheese. Instead, she incorporated a savory brûlée mix. The dish was always moist and flavorful, and in spite of the fact that it contains absolutely no processed cheeses like Velveeta, we still got the kids to eat it as long as we did not add the Scotch bonnet chili peppers to theirs. Here is my version of Dorit's recipe.

1 cup brunoised yellow onion
2 tablespoons minced garlic
½ cup brunoised carrots
¼ cup Herb Butter (page 27)
⅓ cup ketchup
4 tablespoons Dijon mustard
2 tablespoons kosher salt
⅓ cup fresh thyme leaves
½ teaspoon smoked paprika
1 teaspoon Scotch bonnet hot sauce
   (optional)
1 quart heavy cream
10 whole eggs
1 cup grated Parmesan
1 cup grated cheddar cheese, divided
1 pound penne pasta, cooked al dente
   according to directions on package
1 cup small-diced plum tomatoes

1 cup grated Comté cheese
½ cup crushed Ritz crackers

Preheat oven to 380°F. Make sure the rack is in the middle of the oven. Prepare a large baking dish either by spraying with Pam or rubbing with butter.

In a 6-quart stockpot over medium-high heat, sauté onion, garlic and carrots in butter until tender. Add ketchup, mustard, salt, thyme, paprika and hot sauce and stir. Add heavy cream and bring to a boil. Lower to a simmer and cook for 5 minutes, then remove from heat.

Meanwhile, in a large stainless-steel bowl, beat eggs with a whisk. Slowly drizzle cream mixture into eggs, tempering them. Whisk in Parmesan and ½ cup cheddar. Fold in cooked pasta and the tomatoes.

Using your hands, transfer half the pasta mix into the baking dish. Sprinkle remaining cheddar and ½ cup Comté on top. Cover with more pasta mix and pour remaining cream over it, almost to the rim. Top with remaining Comté and the cracker crumbs, cover with foil, and bake for 40 minutes.

Uncover and check that edges are cooked. Continue cooking, uncovered, until center has solidified, is firm to the touch and cooked through, about 10 minutes.

Serves 8 to 10

✳ If there is any cream mixture remaining in the stainless-steel bowl, save it in an airtight container in the refrigerator. It can be used the following day

to reheat leftovers by placing mac 'n' cheese in a smaller baking dish, pouring cream over macaroni and baking for about 20 minutes at 375°F.

Boniato-Sweet Plantain Mash

Living in South Florida, I have access to many tropical and subtropical types of produce. It is definitely an ethnic melting pot here, and with the influx of so many cultures comes a wide variety of fruits and vegetables brought from other countries. I love the combination of boniato and its starchy creaminess, the bright orange color of sweet potato that adds all those great vitamins, and the sweet yet lemony flavor of plantain that marries so well with citrus and cinnamon. This is a light, healthy side that pairs well with Berkshire Pork Tenderloin in Pomelo-Coriander Mojo with Citrus-Braised Onions (page 180), Pan-Roasted Duck Breast with Mango-Cherry Chili Chutney Sauce (page 174) or even my Seasonal Pan-Seared Black Grouper with Buttered Chayote and Carrots in a Bacardi Limón Sauce (page 142).

2 (about 2½ pounds) peeled and
   quartered boniato (place in cold
   water, as it discolors quickly)
1 large Garnet sweet potato,
   peeled and quartered
2 sweet plantains
   (should be soft with mottled dark skin)
2 oranges, washed and cut in half
3 lemons, washed and cut in half
1 cinnamon stick
½ cup freshly squeezed orange juice

¼ cup freshly squeezed lemon juice
½ cup Sugar in the Raw (or to taste)
½ ground cinnamon
2 tablespoons kosher salt
½ stick salted butter

In a large pot, boil water and add boniato, sweet potato, plantains, oranges, lemons and cinnamon stick. Cook until tender and then strain.

Discard cinnamon stick and citrus peels, then place in the bowl of an electric mixer or food processor. (If using a food processor, you may need to divide into 2 batches.) While mixing, slowly feed in juices, sugar, cinnamon salt and butter. Purée until a smooth mashed-potato consistency. Taste for flavor and the balance of sweetness and salt.

❋ You may want to Google what a boniato looks like, because it is called different names by different nationalities. It usually has a deep maroon, almost purple, flaky-looking skin, but can vary in color. It is less sweet and less wet than what we know in the U.S. as a sweet potato. It can be fibrous, which is why I like to put it through a food processor when mixing.

Serves 6 to 8

Fig-Walnut Potato Gratin

This gratin is certainly a bit different, and definitely a touch elegant. I decided to feature this recipe as one of my side dishes because it is just a little out of the normal range of your average potato gratin. It goes beautifully with the Mesquite Coffee- and Cocoa-Rubbed Domestic Rack of Lamb (page 206), as well as a substitue for the butter beans and grape tomatoes over truffled gnocchi in the Port-Braised Certified Angus Beef Short Ribs (page 209). When serving this, it is always so gratifying to watch the gusto with which your guests savor this dish.

6 tablespoons salted butter
1½ cups brunoised yellow onion
4 large cloves garlic, minced
1 vanilla bean
2 cups heavy cream
½ teaspoon freshly grated nutmeg
2 tablespoons fresh thyme leaves
4 tablespoons kosher salt, divided
2 pints ripe sweet figs
    (Turkish, Black Mission or Kadota,
    whichever are sweetest or in season)
3 tablespoons brown sugar
1½ cups chopped walnuts
5 large eggs
3½–4 pounds Yukon Gold potatoes,
    sliced thin on mandoline and
    placed in water to keep from
    discoloring
1 cup white cheddar cheese
1 cup Stilton cheese
¾ cup grated Parmesan cheese
1 teaspoon freshly grated
    black pepper

Preheat oven to 375°F. Make sure the rack is in the center. Prepare a 9-by-13-inch baking dish either by spraying with Pam or rubbing with butter.

In a 6-quart stockpot over medium-high heat, melt butter and sauté onion and garlic until tender. Do not brown them; you may have to lower heat a little if they begin to caramelize.

Split vanilla bean down the center lengthwise, scrape out seeds with a knife and add them, along with the pod, to onion and garlic. Add cream, then nutmeg, thyme, and 3 tablespoons salt. Stir and cook over medium heat.

Cut stems off figs, slice in half and place in a bowl. Toss in brown sugar and remaining salt. Add walnuts and mix. Set aside.

Raise heat and bring cream mixture to a boil. As soon as it boils, turn off heat.

In a very large stainless-steel bowl, beat eggs.

Drain potatoes and pat dry.

Add cheddar to cream mixture and stir. Carefully drizzle hot cream into eggs while whisking, tempering the eggs. Once all cream has been transferred, add potatoes.

Place ⅓ of the potatoes in the baking dish. Sprinkle ½ cup Stilton cheese on top of the first layer of potatoes. At this point, the dish should be half-full.

Scatter all figs and nuts on top of the cheese layer. Add another ⅓ potatoes, then remaining Stilton. Finish with remaining potatoes and sprinkle Parmesan all over the top.

Cover with foil and bake for about 45 minutes. After 45 minutes, use a knife to check that potatoes are tender. Uncover and cook 10 minutes more or until cheese has browned. Let gratin rest for 10 to 15 minutes before cutting.

Serves 8 to 10

continued on page 196

continued from page 195

Creamed Corn and Manchego Cheese Polenta

4 tablespoons salted butter

½ cup minced shallots

2 cloves fresh garlic, minced

4 cups chicken stock

1 bunch fresh thyme, tied

2 tablespoons fresh thyme leaves

2 ears corn, cut off cob
    (reserve cobs to flavor chicken stock)

½ cup heavy cream

Kosher salt and freshly ground
    black pepper, to taste

1½ cups high-quality coarse-grain
    polenta (I recommend Moretti
    Bramata or other not-instant brand)

¾ cup grated Manchego cheese

In a 6-quart saucepan, melt butter and sweat shallots and garlic over medium heat. Add stock, tied thyme and corncobs and bring to a boil. Boil stock until reduced by almost 1 cup. Turn off the heat and remove thyme and cobs with tongs and discard. Measure stock; it should be close to 3 cups. (When cooking polenta, you should always have a bit of extra hot stock just in case, as different brands require more or less liquid. Read the back of the box or bag that you purchase for the proper ratio.) After measuring, return to saucepan and begin heating again.

In a small saucepan over medium-high heat, place heavy cream, corn, salt and pepper. Bring to a boil, then immediately add to stock. Stir.

When mixture is almost boiling, add polenta. Stir constantly with a whisk, making sure there are no lumps. Lower to a simmer.

Although you do not have to stand there the whole time watching it (as long as you keep it on a very low flame), you should not go far. You can continue to prep the rest of your meal, but stir polenta intermittently. Watch for polenta thickening too much, adding a little more hot chicken stock if necessary. Once polenta is tender and not grainy, about 40 minutes if using slow-cooking polenta, whisk in cheese and turn off the heat.

Season to taste and serve immediately.

Serves 8

Parmesan Oven-Roasted Spaghetti Squash

One of my favorite vegetables, spaghetti squash is simple to make and also happens to be a great substitute for pasta, and is very low in carbs. Like pasta, cook it on the al dente side and toss with a great olive oil and Parmigiano-Reggiano.

1 large spaghetti squash,
    cut in half lengthwise and seeded

4 tablespoons olive oil, divided

1 tablespoon kosher salt

Freshly ground black pepper, to taste

¼ cup high-quality extra virgin olive oil

¼ cup minced shallots

2 tablespoons minced garlic

1 tablespoons Maldon salt

¼ cup chopped parsley

½ cup grated Parmesan

Preheat oven to 400°F.

With a fork, scrape flesh of squash just a bit and rub it with 2 tablespoons olive oil. Sprinkle with kosher salt and desired amount of pepper. Place halves, flesh side down, on a baking dish. Add about ½ cup water to the baking dish (this helps steam the squash a bit) and place on the middle rack in the oven. Bake for about 30 minutes.

Remove from oven and poke with fork. If squash is tender, turn off oven and set aside. Once cool enough to handle, use a fork to pull squash out of shell in strands.

Meanwhile, heat a skillet over medium with 1 tablespoon olive oil and sauté shallots and garlic until tender. Raise heat to high and add squash and remaining oil, Maldon salt and parsley.

Once hot, remove from heat and toss in a bowl with Parmesan. Enjoy with protein or pasta sauce of your choice.

Serves 4

Grilled Corn on the Cob in the Husk

Growing up in New Jersey, we had the sweetest, most wonderful corn there was. During the summer months—corn season—there was not one night that Mom didn't have corn on our table. It was the only time Green Giant Niblets was overridden for the real thing. But it was on Mount Diablo, in Jamaica, with my then-husband, Charles Hutson, that I had this particular style of corn, steamed in its own husk. The corn was a bit tougher there, what Mom and Dad would have called "cow corn," being the Jersey corn (and tomato) snobs they were. Still, I am sure even they would have loved this flavorful Jamaican corn preparation.

6 ears corn, unpeeled
1 bunch thyme
2 bunches scallions
8 cloves fresh garlic,
    smashed with flat side of knife
8 allspice berries, cracked
2 Red Stripe beers
3 tablespoons kosher salt
1–2 Scotch bonnet chili peppers,
    seeded and diced
    (can substitute jalapeños)
Enough water to cover

Husk outer green leaves of corn, making sure you have at least 2 or 3 layers of green leaves remaining. Very carefully, peel them away from corn, exposing the silk. Remove as much silk as possible without ripping off any more outer leaves. Press green leaves back into place on corn.

In a pot or a bowl big enough to hold corn, place all seasonings and beer. Add corn and any water (or more beer) needed to cover corn. Keep corn submerged, soaking for at least 1 hour.

Prepare and heat a grill. Place corn, with husks, on the grates. (You can place some of the thyme, garlic and other marinade spices inside the husks for additional flavor while cooking.) As husks begin to smoke and

burn, turn corn. Repeat until all sides are cooked.

Remove from grill. Serve with Herb Butter (page 27) and sea salt.

Serves 6

✳ If you don't have a grill or if you live in an apartment, you can soak the corn for 1 hour and then just cook the corn in that soaking liquid. Bring to a boil and then immediately remove from heat. Using tongs, pull out the corn and let husks drip into pot. Carefully place in a baking dish. Discard husks and serve with Herb Butter and sea salt as above.

Sautéed Jamaican Callaloo

Callaloo is a green, large leafy plant, originating in South Africa. It is very high in calcium, iron and potassium. Unlike our more familiar spinach, it does not shrink down to almost nothing when cooked. It is firmer and has less water content than spinach, so basically if you cook 1 cup callaloo, you wind up with ¾ cup callaloo. It is definitely one of my favorite vegetables, earthy and flavorful. It is the base of my Traditional "Peppa" Pot Soup (page 36), but its contribution to a great recipe does not stop there. If you are fortunate enough to be able to find and purchase it in the U.S., do try it, but if you can't, substitute with kale, which is a close second.

1–1½ pounds fresh callaloo bunch,
    washed and woody stem cut off
¼ cup olive oil
1 cup brunoised yellow onion

4 cloves fresh garlic, minced
¾ cup brunoised carrot
2 tablespoons kosher salt
1 teaspoon chopped fresh
    Scotch bonnet chili pepper
    (or bottled sauce)
¾ cup brunoised tomatoes,
    as few seeds as possible
½ cup fresh thyme leaves

Cut up callaloo into small pieces, keeping larger stem pieces to one side. Have a boiling pot of salted water ready to blanch the stems for 1 minute alone. Then add the remaining chopped callaloo and cook for 3 minutes. Strain the callaloo and plunge into ice bath. Strain callaloo again from the cold water. It is now ready to sauté.

In a large, deep sauté pan over medium-high heat, sauté onion and garlic in oil until tender. If too hot and onion begins to brown, lower heat. Add carrot and continue to sauté. Add salt and Scotch bonnet.

After about 5 minutes, add blanched callaloo and mix thoroughly. With heat on medium, cover pan and let it steam for 4 to 5 minutes. Uncover and stir in tomatoes and thyme. Taste and reseason with salt and pepper if necessary.

Serve immediately.

Serves 6

✳ You may actually find canned callaloo in some places where you can't find fresh, but I don't recommend using it. It's not the same. In fact, it's like buying canned spinach. Need I say more?

Braised Beef Cheeks
with Farro and Wild Mushroom Pappardelle Pasta

Pappardelle is definitely one of my favorite pastas. It is hearty and can stand up to decadent sauces or gamey meats. Although beef cheeks are not gamey, they are rich and a bit out of the ordinary for a home cook to use. The cheeks of beef, veal or pork are very easy to prepare and usually quite affordable. I have chosen beef cheeks for this recipe because it's a perfect recipe to experiment with a cut of meat you may not ordinarily use. When you go to the butcher to buy your beef cheeks, ask him to clean them of the silver skin and the fatty tissue connected to them. (Always develop a friendly relationship with your local butcher—you will be surprised what they can teach you about cuts of meat!)

SERVES SIX TO EIGHT

Braised Beef Cheeks

3 pounds beef cheeks
Salt and freshly ground black pepper, to taste
6 tablespoons olive oil
4 allspice berries
2 whole cloves garlic
10 cloves garlic, smashed
1 large onion, diced
2 celery stalks, sliced
1½ cups diced carrots
¼ cup tomato paste
1 cup chopped tomatoes
1 bunch thyme
2 cups dry red wine
2 tablespoons kosher salt

Farro and Wild Mushroom Pappardelle Pasta

¾ cup high-quality olive oil
¾ cup thinly sliced garlic
½ cup minced shallots
1 cup sliced cremini mushrooms
1 cup sliced morels
   (or substitute your favorite seasonal mushrooms)
1 cup sliced chanterelles
   (or substitute your favorite seasonal mushrooms)
1 cup good white wine
1½ cups farro, cooked according to directions
   on package, slightly al dente
¾ cup heavy cream

continued on page 200

continued from page 198

2 bunches escarole, soaked in ice water
to remove sand, cleaned and chopped
Prepared braised beef cheeks (recipe above)
1½ pounds high-quality pappardelle, cooked al dente
(it will finish cooking during preparation)
½ cup chopped parsley
1 cup pecorino cheese
Salt and pepper, to taste

Prepare braised beef cheeks

Preheat oven to 350°F. Make sure rack is in center of oven.

Season beef cheeks on both sides with salt and pepper. In a Dutch oven over medium-high heat, warm olive oil. Add beef cheeks, allspice and whole cloves garlic and brown cheeks for 5 minutes on each side. Remove from pan, place in a bowl and set aside.

In the same Dutch oven, cook smashed garlic, onion, celery and carrots over medium heat, sautéing continuously. If pan is too hot, lower the heat so that you do not scorch the vegetables.

Once tender, add tomato paste and chopped tomatoes. Stir for a minute and then add wine. Bring to a boil and return the cheeks and any juices back to the pot. You may need to add a cup or so of beef stock so that there is enough liquid to almost cover the cheeks.

Cover the pot and place in oven. Cook for about 3 hours, until the cheeks are very tender. When done, strain cooking liquid into a pot, bring to a boil and then simmer until reduced to about 2½ cups. Reserve. This is the sauce for your pasta ingredients.

Prepare farro and wild mushroom pappardelle pasta

In a deep skillet, heat olive oil over a low flame and sauté garlic and shallots for 4 minutes. Add mushrooms and sauté for 2 to 3 minutes; do not overcook. Remove mushrooms with a slotted spoon, place in a bowl and set aside.

Add wine and simmer over medium heat for about 4 minutes. Add 1½ cups reserved beef cheek sauce and simmer for 5 minutes. Add cooked farro, thyme and heavy cream and simmer until cream begins to thicken.

Add cooked pappardelle, the mushrooms and their liquid, and escarole. Continue to cook over low heat. Toss, add beef and toss again (meat will be tender and tear apart while tossing). Remove from heat and toss again with parsley, pecorino, and salt and pepper. Divide among 6 to 8 bowls and serve.

 If you have a little white truffle oil, it tastes very nice drizzled on the pasta just before serving.

Jerk-Brined "T-Bone" Pork Chop in Bacardi Oakheart Guava Sauce

with Tropical Fruit Flambé

Back in 1998, when Delius and I had Norma's on the Beach, someone from the National Pork Board came in and asked me to participate in a competition against 35 other chefs with a T-bone pork chop I had on my menu. Much like a beef T-bone, this is a center-cut pork loin on one side and a piece of tenderloin on the other, separated by a little "T" of bone. I love this cut thick, 1¾ inches, and I think it's at its best when it's brined and cooked medium-rare to medium. The Bacardi Oakheart sauce comes into play because of its compatibility with Jamaican jerk seasoning. The rum has a sweetness that balances the heat of the Scotch bonnet in the jerk. It has subtle flavors of cinnamon, nutmeg and allspice, which are also strong, complementary jerk spices. Brine this, throw it on a grill and don't forget to shake a rum cocktail to go with it, because that's a match made in heaven.

Incidentally, I came in first place, winning $2,000 and gaining recognition as one of the Pork Board's "Celebrated Chefs" Taste of Elegance. It was a very significant moment of validation for me.

SERVES FOUR

Jerk-Brined Pork Chop

4 (14–16 ounces) center-cut (T-bone in) pork chops
1 recipe Jerk Brine (page 159)
1 recipe Jerk Paste (page 145), optional
¼ cup Clarified Butter (page 27)

2 cups Bacardi Oakheart Guava Sauce
 (recipe next page)
2½ cups Tropical Fruit Flambé (recipe next page)

continued on page 204

continued from page 202

Bacardi Oakheart Guava Sauce

8 tablespoons (1 stick) salted butter
4 cups sliced sweet yellow onion
1 cup Bacardi Oakheart rum
10 ounces guava paste
   (Goya is the brand with the richest flavor)
2 cups water
2 cups chicken stock
¾ cup Busha Browne's Planters Steak Sauce
   (substitute Pickapeppa Sauce or,
   as a last resort, A.1. Bold & Spicy)

Tropical Fruit Flambé

¾ cup raisins
¾ cup Bacardi Gold
3 tablespoons salted butter
1½ cups diced mango
1½ cups diced papaya

Prepare jerk-brined pork chop

Place jerk brine in a bowl and add pork chops. Brine in the refrigerator for at least 2 hours or overnight. After pork has been brined, remove and discard brine.

Now, in another bowl, place jerk paste and marinate pork for another hour, this time at room temperature. If you don't want the extra spice, skip this step.

Prepare your grill and heat it to about 425°F. Place chops on the grill and cook for 5 to 8 minutes on one side. Flip and finish cooking until desired doneness. I prefer to cook them to an internal tempera-ture of 135° to 140°F. Remove from heat and let rest for 10 minutes before serving.

Serve chops with guava sauce and top with flambé.

Prepare Bacardi Oakheart guava sauce

In a medium saucepan, melt butter and sauté onions. Stir occasionally, taking care not to burn. When cara-melized, add rum and simmer for 3 minutes.

Add guava paste and stir. Add water and simmer 5 minutes. Add stock and bring to a rolling boil, and then lower heat to medium-high.

Add steak sauce and stir. Maintain a strong simmer for 15 to 20 minutes, until sauce has been reduced by one-quarter.

Remove from heat and slowly pour into a blender. Remove plastic center piece of the blender lid and place the top on the blender. Hold a kitchen towel over the hole, making sure the lid is secure. Pulse blender a couple times to release steam, then blend steadily for 3 minutes on high or until sauce is smooth in consistency.

Makes about 1 quart

Prepare tropical fruit flambé

In a bowl, place raisins and cover with Bacardi Gold. Soak overnight.

Heat a large sauté pan over medium-high heat. Melt butter and add the fruits. Be careful of the rum flaming. Sauté until rum is cooked off.

Makes 2¾ cups

Amarena Cherry-Chipotle Demi-Glace

2 lamb shanks

Kosher salt and freshly ground
   black pepper, to taste

4 tablespoons Herb Butter (page 27)

1 large yellow onion, chopped

6 cloves fresh garlic,
   smashed with flat side of knife

2 carrots, chopped

3 sprigs fresh rosemary

¼ cup tomato paste

1 cup brandy

3 quarts homemade veal stock
   (substitute 2 quarts made
   from Demi-Glace Gold)

1½ cups chopped Amarena cherries
   in syrup (canned or bottled)

2 chipotle peppers in adobo sauce
   (canned), remove as many seeds
   as possible

Preheat oven to 400°F.

Rub lamb shanks with kosher salt and pepper, then roast on a baking sheet in oven until browned. Remove and set aside.

In a saucepan over medium heat, sauté onions and garlic in Herb Butter until caramelized. Add carrots, rosemary and tomato paste and stir for about 2 minutes. Add brandy, roasted lamb shanks and veal stock. If lamb shanks are not covered, add a little water just to cover. Bring to a boil and then reduce to a strong simmer. Simmer for about 1 hour, until lamb is tender.

Remove from heat and strain. Reserve the lamb shanks for another recipe or eat as a snack. Return stock to saucepan and bring back to a strong simmer. Add cherries and chipotle and simmer until sauce begins to thicken. Using a 4-ounce ladle, skim off any fat or impurities

Demi-Glaces and Glazes

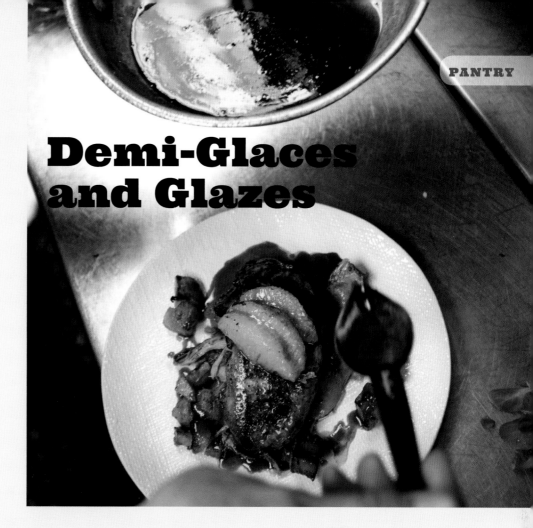

that rise to the top and discard. Taste and season if necessary.

✱ Although this demi-glace is fairly versatile and can pair with anything from dark poultry—think ostrich!—to a veal chop, in this book I showcase it with the Mesquite Coffee- and Cocoa-Rubbed Domestic Rack of Lamb (page 206).

Chipotle Agave Glaze

2 cups freshly squeezed orange juice

2 chipotle peppers in adobo sauce
   (canned)

2 cups agave nectar

1 cup honey

2 tablespoons orange zest

In a small saucepan, place orange juice and peppers. Bring to a roll-

ing simmer and reduce by half. Add agave, honey and orange zest. Stir and simmer for 20 to 30 minutes. Once a syrupy consistency, the sauce is ready.

Strain through a fine-mesh sieve, pushing against peppers, into an airtight container. This sauce keeps for months stored in the refrigerator.

Makes about 3 cups

✱ Easy and quick to make, a little of this glaze goes a long way on lighter game meats, poultry and fish. But you'd be surprised what happens when you also pair it with some of the rubs—say, the Mesquite Coffee and Cocoa Rub (page 145)—and short ribs. It's an unusual and delicious combination!

Mesquite Coffee- and Cocoa-Rubbed Domestic Rack of Lamb

in Amarena Cherry-Chipotle Demi-Glace

I have prepared this dish for many wine dinners, as it pairs beautifully with full-bodied, richly endowed red wines. Coffee, cocoa, orange and the smokiness of chipotle are made for each other. They also echo the aromatics found in good red wines. Try it yourself with a variety of wines at home—you'll be pleased with the results. As for the lamb, ask your butcher to pick you out a heavy domestic lamb rack and figure on two chops per person. Sometimes it is a nine-bone rack, but most times it is eight. If your butcher likes you, he will French it and trim the fat cap a bit; otherwise, it's all up to you. Just another reason to find yourself a good artisan butcher and make friends.

SERVES TWO TO FOUR

1 heavy (26–30 ounce) domestic lamb rack, frenched
2 tablespoons olive oil
1 recipe Mesquite Coffee and Cocoa Rub (page 145)
4–6 tablespoons Clarified Butter
   (page 27) (can substitute high-quality oil)
1 recipe Amarena Cherry–Chipotle Demi-Glace
   (page 205)

Make sure a baking rack is in the middle of the oven. Preheat oven to 450°F.

Rub lamb rack with olive oil and sprinkle mesquite rub everywhere, pressing the rub into the meat.

Take a piece of aluminum foil a little longer than the rack of lamb and, at the edge of where the meat turns to bone, place the end of the foil and wrap the exposed lamb bones so they do not burn during the cooking process. Then set aside and bring to room temperature before roasting.

In an ovenproof skillet large enough to hold the lamb rack, preferably a cast iron or black steel pan, heat butter over high heat. You need to see it sizzle around the rack when searing.

Sear rack, fat side down, until a nice golden-brown color, about 4 minutes, then flip and do the same for the second side.

Flip again and transfer to oven. Finish cooking to the desired temperature; I recommend medium-rare or an internal temperature of 125° to 130°F on a meat thermometer.

Remove lamb from oven when it reaches 120°F internally and let rest for 10 minutes before cutting (the temperature will rise 5 to 10 degrees).

Portion lamb into 2 or 4 servings. Drizzle with the demi-glace and serve.

Port-Braised Certified Angus Beef Short Ribs

with Butter Beans and Grape Tomatoes over Truffled Gnocchi

Short ribs are delicious, but very fatty. I guess that's why they taste so great! They do shrink quite a lot when you cook them, though, so buy a bit more than you think you need. I like braising short ribs best because then I can scrape out some of the excess fat easily before serving them. This gnocchi recipe comes out really nicely too, with the pungency of the Parmesan in the dough. As you pan-sear them in the clarified butter, they crisp nicely around the edges, giving the fluffy inside texture a great contrast. This is another recipe where leftovers are always welcome. Both the short ribs and the gnocchi freeze well and keep for weeks, reheating beautifully for the next time you crave them.

SERVES EIGHT

Port-Braised Certified Angus Beef Short Ribs

1 recipe Cumin and Coriander Spice Rub
    (page 145)
2 pounds (3 bone-in) short ribs
½ cup olive oil
3 cups coarsely chopped onions, skin on
6 cloves garlic, peeled and smashed
2 cups coarsely chopped celery
3 cups coarsely chopped carrots
10 whole allspice berries
1 cup tomato paste
2 whole stars anise
½ bottle port
    (substitute Cabernet Sauvignon or any good red wine)
1 bunch fresh thyme, left whole, but bruise by twisting
3 bay leaves
1 Scotch bonnet chili pepper (optional)
2 tablespoons kosher salt
8 cups beef stock
Salt and pepper, to taste
1 can butter beans, drained
1 pint grape tomatoes, halved lengthwise
Chopped parsley, for garnish

Truffled Gnocchi

2½ pounds whole Russet potatoes, skin on
3 large egg yolks
⅓ cup freshly grated Parmesan cheese
1 cup all-purpose flour, plus more as needed
2 tablespoons kosher salt, plus more to taste
⅓ cup canned black truffle shavings,
    drained and roughly chopped
1 tablespoon white truffle oil
1 recipe Clarified Butter (page 27)

Prepare port-braised Certified Angus Beef short ribs

Preheat oven to 400°F.

Place short-rib racks on a roasting pan large enough to hold all of them. Rub spices into top of meat. Turn over and sprinkle the underside too.

Place in oven, bone side down, and roast until ribs begin to get golden brown and a little crispy, about 20 minutes. Remove from oven and set meat aside. Discard any excess short-rib fat remaining in the pan.

Lower oven to 325°F.

In the roasting pan, over high heat on the stove, add

continued on page 210

continued from page 209

olive oil and sauté onions, garlic, celery, carrots and allspice berries for about 4 minutes.

Add tomato paste and star anise. Cook, stirring, for about 5 minutes.

Add port, stir, then add bay leaves, thyme, Scotch bonnet and salt. Add short ribs to the mixture and cover with beef stock. If stock doesn't cover the meat, add water until it does. Bring to a boil, then turn off the flame and remove.

Cover roasting pan with foil and place in oven. Cook for 2½ hours or until the bone slips from the meat easily.

Remove from oven and let cool, then remove meat from the braising liquids, reserving liquids. Slightly trim off fat. Cut into 8 portions and set aside.

Strain liquids into a pot and simmer for at least 45 minutes, until the consistency of syrup. Season with salt and pepper.

In a sauté pan, heat short ribs in their braising sauce and add some grape tomatoes and the butter beans. Taste for seasoning and adjust if necessary.

Prepare truffled gnocchi

Preheat oven to 350°F. Cook potatoes in oven for 1 hour or until fork-tender.

Remove from oven. When potatoes are cool enough to handle, split them, remove flesh and press the flesh through a ricer.

Place riced potato in a pile on a clean table. Make a well in the middle and add egg yolks, cheese, flour and salt. Then, using a dough scraper, fold potato into the well until the ingredients are mixed. This process should be done quickly so you do not overwork the potatoes into starchiness. You can add more flour if needed.

Add truffles and truffle oil and quickly incorporate. If a little more flour is needed, add so that the dough is not tacky. Shape into a ball and sprinkle some extra flour on the surface, then roll into logs the size of long cigars. With the dough scraper, break off 1-inch pieces.

Boil a pot of salted water and prepare an ice bath. Drop about 20 gnocchi into boiling water. When they float, which is almost immediately, they are done. Remove with a slotted spoon and drop into the ice bath, then do another batch.

In a hot sauté pan, heat butter and sauté the finished gnocchi until golden brown. Divide among 6 to 8 plates and then top each with about 4 squares of short-rib meat. Spoon some beef sauce, beans and tomatoes on the plate and garnish with parsley.

Any leftover gnocchi not used can be frozen for future use. Any extra short ribs are great served the next day as sliders.

CHAPTER 8

DESSEI

RTS

Making desserts is not really my "thing." Having said that, though, and looking back, sweets were the first things I cooked as a child. I was nine years old when I stood on a stool, reading the back of a Bisquick box, where there was a recipe for pineapple upside-down cake. Naturally, I made it. It was awesome! I thought I was Julia Child. Next, with confidence bursting at the seams, I made the best butter chocolate fudge from the box of Baker's chocolate. My mom and I ate the whole 9-by-13-inch pan. Today, I try to stay away from those calories, but whenever I do invent a dessert, it's not science. What I mean by that is that it's not always about exact measurements. The recipe is more like how I cook savory items—I start with a little of this, then add a little of that. There's the comfort, there's something warm, then ice cream usually follows somehow, and so on, until it's worth the calories. For all other desserts, I rely on my wonderful pastry chefs. So I thank my girls Monica, Quiana, Kelli and Barbara for contributing to this chapter. Love them, even though my hips don't!

Drunken Banana Fritters

with Cinnamon Ice Cream
and Rum-Soaked
Raisin Whipped Cream

This was my first original restaurant dessert, served at Norma's on the Beach. Customers loved it, so I took it with me to every restaurant we opened, where it was always the top-selling dessert. Every pastry chef scowled at me, though, because the batter was almost impossible to stick on those rum-soaked bananas. Finally, at Ortanique on the Mile, I had to take them off the menu because the fire department said I didn't have the right hood in the pastry station for the fryers, and I could no longer cook them. Customers said they would boycott. No, really; they were irate. I still hear about it today. I even heard about the displeasure of a Coral Gables fireman whose name remains anonymous. So you see, even at home, they are worth the hassle.

SERVES SIX

Rum-Soaked Raisins

¾ cup raisins
⅓ cup dark rum

Fritter Batter

2 eggs, whites and yolks separated
1 tablespoon sugar
½ teaspoon kosher salt
2 tablespoons salted butter, melted
3 cups all-purpose flour
1½ cups light beer

Rum-Raisin Whipped Cream

1 pint very cold heavy cream
¾ cup Rum-Soaked Raisins
1 tablespoon vanilla extract
1 tablespoon sugar

Cinnamon Sugar

3 tablespoons ground cinnamon
¾ cup sugar

Drunken Bananas

½ cup dark rum
¼ cup brown sugar
1 tablespoon ground cinnamon
4 ripe bananas, cut in half lengthwise
   and then in half horizontally
1 quart store-bought cinnamon ice cream

Prepare rum-soaked raisins

In a bowl, combine raisins and dark rum. Allow raisins to soak at least 30 minutes or overnight.

Prepare fritter batter

In a large mixing bowl, beat egg yolks with sugar, salt and butter. Add flour and beer and gently combine.

In a separate bowl, whip egg whites until stiff. Fold them into the batter. Set aside for at least 30 minutes before using.

Makes 1 quart

continued on page 216

continued from page 215

Prepare rum-raisin whipped cream

Place cream in the freezer for 15 minutes before whipping.

Transfer cream to a blender. Turn it on the slowest speed and begin blending. As soon as you see the cream begin to thicken, turn off blender and add rum-soaked raisins, vanilla extract and sugar. Stir.

Resume blending, a little faster this time, watching carefully. As it thickens a bit and raisins blend in, stop it once again, stir, and restart.

At this point, it is close to finished. Watch carefully as it thickens. Stop blending as soon as you see it reach the thickness of whipped cream. Do not over-whip. Place it into a bowl and refrigerate until ready to top fritters.

Makes 2 cups

Prepare cinnamon sugar

In a small bowl, combine cinnamon and sugar. Set aside until fritters are fried. If you run out while coating fritters, simply repeat this recipe.

Makes about 1 cup

Prepare drunken bananas

In a small bowl, combine rum, sugar and cinnamon. Add bananas and allow to macerate for at least 30 minutes.

Prepare a deep fryer. Add frying oil according to the manufacturer's recommended fill-to line, and heat to 325°F.

Coat marinated bananas in the fritter batter. This can be tricky, as it is a thick batter and sometimes it almost needs to be wrapped around the banana. Don't get frustrated; you've almost reached the final prize. One by one, drop fritters into the fryer.

As fritters turn golden brown, remove them and let the oil drip off a little into the fryer. Then toss them in the cinnamon sugar to coat. Keep warm until you have fried all the bananas.

Divide among 6 bowls, giving each bowl at least 2 fritters. Serve with a scoop of cinnamon ice cream and top with the raisin whipped cream.

✳ Yes, these bananas are time consuming. Yes, they can be frustrating. But they are truly worth it. I do recommend a Presto FryDaddy to fry these, as a pot with oil is just too hard to keep consistent heatwise. Good luck!

Lavender Panna Cotta
with Macadamia Honey and Moscato Drizzle

Panna cotta is so versatile. It can be savory or sweet, and you can be very creative using different flavor profiles. With this one, though, be careful not to put too much lavender in it, or you will feel like you are eating massage oil.

SERVES EIGHT TO TEN, DEPENDING ON HOW HIGH YOU FILL THE RAMEKINS

Lavender Panna Cotta

1⅔ cups whole milk
2 cups heavy cream
1 cup sugar
4½ sheets gelatin
½ vanilla bean, insides scraped
¼ cup dried lavender flowers, wrapped in cheesecloth

Moscato Drizzle

2 bottles Moscato wine
1 cup light brown sugar
½ cup macadamia honey
2 teaspoons orange zest

Prepare lavender panna cotta

Grease 8 to 10 4-ounce foil ramekins. You can buy these in the grocery store.

In a heavy-bottom saucepan, heat milk, cream, sugar, vanilla and lavender-filled cheesecloth to a boil. Reduce to a simmer and add gelatin.

Let steep for about 10 minutes. Squeeze out cheesecloth into the mixture and remove.

Pour mixture into prepared ramekins and refrigerate for at least 2 to 3 hours, until set.

Prepare Moscato drizzle

In a heavy-bottom saucepan, heat all ingredients over a medium-high flame. Reduce until mixture becomes syrupy. Stir occasionally. Once it coats a spoon, it is done.

Allow sauce to cool to at least room temperature so it does not melt the panna cotta.

To serve the panna cotta, run a thin knife along the inside rim of the foil, then turn the foil ramekin upside down on a plate and poke a hole in the bottom of it. The panna cotta will fall out. Top with Moscato drizzle and serve while still chilled.

✳ **Macadamia honey can be purchased online or in high-end specialty stores. It works well with the lavender flavor. If you can't find it, avocado or blueberry honeys are good substitutes. If those also fail you, fall back on clover honey, which is available everywhere.**

✳ **To add color and another level of flavor, marinate seasonal strawberries with orange zest and vanilla bean flecks, then use for a garnish—delish!**

Heath Bar Bread Pudding

with Toffee Sauce

One afternoon I had to make a special dessert on the fly. In fact, I had to put together a whole menu that way. In restaurant lingo, *on the fly* means really fast, no questions asked. One of our regular customers had told his wife that at his request, Chef Cindy was making her a special anniversary menu designed especially for them. Only problem was, he had forgotten to inform me until two and a half hours before their arrival. I had to think of a quick dessert, easy to put together, something warm and gooey that would cause a closed-eye, "Mmm-good" reaction. This was it.

SERVES EIGHT TO TEN

Heath Bar Bread Pudding

4 cups heavy whipping cream

1¼ cups sugar

1 tablespoon vanilla extract

10 egg yolks

10 cups brioche bread, cubed and left out
   the night before

1 cup Heath candy bar, crumbled

Toffee Sauce

1 cup (2 sticks) unsalted butter

3 cups firmly packed dark muscovado sugar
   (or substitute dark brown sugar)

2 cups heavy cream

1 teaspoon vanilla extract

¼ teaspoon salt

Prepare bread pudding

Preheat oven to 350°F. Butter a 9-by-13-inch baking dish (Pyrex) or individual 4-ounce foil ramekins.

In a heavy-bottom saucepan, heat cream, sugar and vanilla until almost boiling, then remove from heat.

In a large bowl, whisk egg yolks. While whisking rapidly, slowly drizzle cream mixture into egg yolks, tempering them.

Add dried brioche and toss until the bread absorbs the liquid.

Once mixture has been absorbed and is cool, add most of the chopped Heath bar and mix again. Transfer to the prepared baking dish.

Bake for 20 minutes or until golden brown on top. Stick with a toothpick to test if it is cooked through. If the toothpick comes out clean, the pudding is done.

Keep warm until ready to serve.

Prepare toffee sauce

Combine butter and brown sugar in a saucepan over medium heat. Cook until sugar and butter melt together. Add cream, vanilla and salt. Increase heat to high and bring to a boil. Reduce heat to a simmer and cook, stirring frequently, until the sauce thickens, 6 to 8 minutes.

Divide the warm pudding among 8 to 10 serving dishes. Top each portion with a good amount of toffee sauce. Serve with vanilla or Heath bar ice cream, and garnish with reserved Heath bar crumbles.

Tres Leches
with Mango and Whipped Cream

This *tres leches* came about when Kelli Wright-Morales was my pastry chef at Ortanique. Although she is from the good old US of A, she sure made tres leches as if she were directly from South America. I never really was a fan of this particular dessert until she started adding some of our great Miami mangoes during mango season. We have a mango called honey mango that is awesome when made into a coulis. But any variety of mango tastes like heaven when sliced and arranged over the top of a piece of this cake.

SERVES EIGHT TO TEN

6 large eggs, whites and yolks separated
2 cups sugar
2 cups all-purpose flour
2 teaspoons baking powder
½ cup whole milk
2 teaspoons vanilla extract, divided
2 (14-ounce) cans evaporated milk
2 (14-ounce) cans sweetened condensed milk
2 cups heavy cream
1–2 mangoes, sliced
Whipped cream, for serving

Preheat oven to 350°F. Lightly grease and flour a 9-by-13-inch baking dish and set aside.

In the bowl of an electric mixer, beat egg whites on low speed until soft peaks form. Add sugar gradually with the mixer running and beat to stiff peaks. Add egg yolks 1 at a time, beating well after each.

In a separate bowl, sift together flour and baking powder. Quickly, so batter doesn't lose volume, alternate adding flour mixture and whole milk to the bowl of the running mixer. Add 1 teaspoon vanilla extract and mix one final time. Pour into the prepared baking dish.

Bake until golden and a toothpick inserted into the center comes out clean, about 45 minutes.

Meanwhile, in a blender, combine canned milks, heavy cream and remaining vanilla extract and blend on high speed.

Remove cake from the oven and, while still warm, poke holes in it with a toothpick or fork. Pour condensed milk mixture over it. Let cool to room temperature.

Cover and refrigerate until well-chilled, at least 4 hours or overnight. Serve topped with fresh mango slices and whipped cream.

Peanut Butter Parfait

The Peanut Butter Parfait started out as a slightly different dessert called the Peanut Butter Bomb, created by my chef de cuisine Barbara Scott. It ran on the dessert menus of both Ortanique Miami and Ortanique Grand Cayman, and it was always one of the hits. Then, in one cooking class, I couldn't think up a dessert that could be made in 2 to 3 hours and that didn't require an oven to complete. So I "borrowed" the Bomb, thought about a bunch of toppings or layers that would work in a glass cup, and turned it into the Parfait. This variation is equally delicious, and it's always beautiful.

SERVES EIGHT TO TEN

1½ cups very cold heavy cream, divided
1½ cups creamy peanut butter, room temperature
¼ cup plus 2 tablespoons powdered sugar,
   divided, plus more as needed
1 tablespoon pure vanilla extract
2 cups crushed, roasted, salted peanuts
2 cups crumbled Oreo cookie

Chill a bowl and a pair of an electric mixer's beaters in the refrigerator.

In a different bowl with a different set of beaters, mix peanut butter briefly, until smooth. With the beaters running on low, drizzle ½ cup heavy cream into peanut butter and beat until incorporated.

Add ¼ cup powdered sugar and the vanilla as you continue blending. Once you have a smooth mixture and the peanut butter looks light and airy, stop mixing. Taste, and add more sugar if needed. Once you have reached the desired taste and sweetness, turn mixer on high and beat for about 1 minute, until peanut butter mixture is light and fluffy. Using a spatula, transfer into another mixing bowl and set aside.

Remove the chilled bowl and beaters from the refrigerator and attach to mixer. Whip remaining heavy cream and sugar to make whipped cream. Beat until nice, thick peaks have formed. Do not leave unattended, as overmixing will ruin your parfait.

Using a spatula, gently fold the whipped cream into the peanut butter mixture. Refrain from pushing down on the mixture. You don't want to lose the light, airy, mousse-like texture.

Scoop mixture into a pastry bag with a medium-size hole cut in the bottom. Set out 8 to 10 parfait glasses. Squeeze some mousse into a glass. Layer with cookie crumbles and peanuts, and repeat layering until you fill the glass. Do as many or as few layers as you like. Repeat until all glasses are filled. Chill for at least 2 to 3 hours before serving.

❋ The reason why you chill your bowl and beaters before whipping the cream is that it helps the cream develop structure more quickly. Also, use heavy cream that has at least 36 percent butterfat content. Ultrapasteurized cream does not work as well.

❋ Play with whatever layers you like! Add cake crumbles, pretzels, marshmallows, caramel sauce, brownies, honey-roasted nuts, Rice Krispies, strawberry jam, Nutella—anything that suits your fancy.

Cherries Jubilee

When Delius is given the dessert "chore," this is his go-to, and it's canned all the way: Oregon Fruit brand Bing cherries in syrup. And I have to admit, it's delicious! Plus, it's easy. But as a chef, I had to take it out of the box—or can—a bit. Here it is with the slightly tart and bitter Amarena variety of cherry, which was developed by Gennaro Fabbri in nineteenth-century Bologna, Italy, and is still grown in the Bologna and Modena regions of that country. Like the Bing cherries that Delius uses, imported Amarena cherries are preserved in heavy syrup and canned or jarred. During spring and summer months in the States, replace with fresh Royal Ann cherries.

SERVES SIX

4 tablespoons salted butter
¼ cup sugar
2 tablespoons brown sugar
2 cups Amarena cherries or 1 (15-ounce) can
   Bing cherries, with syrup
1 tablespoon orange zest (no pith)
¼ cup Grand Marnier
¼ teaspoon ground cinnamon
1 tablespoon cornstarch
¼ cup water
1 pint vanilla ice cream
   (or be decadent with Ben & Jerry's Cherry Garcia)
Whipped cream, for topping (optional)

In a large sauté pan, heat butter, then add both sugars. Using a rubber spatula, sauté until sugar has dissolved.

Add cherries and their syrup, the zest, Grand Marnier and cinnamon. Increase heat and bring to a simmer.

Tilt pan toward the flame and allow juices to ignite, burning off the alcohol. As alcohol evaporates, the flame will go out. Then simmer for 4 minutes.

Meanwhile, in a small bowl, mix cornstarch and water to make a slurry. Pour slurry into cherries, stirring continuously until mixture thickens. Remove from heat and allow to cool slightly.

Pour warm cherry compote over your favorite ice cream and top with whipped cream (optional).

❋ **Jars or cans of imported Amarena cherries are sold in most good markets, and you can sometimes find them in liquor stores as well. If you can't locate any nearby, you can always order them online.**

Acknowledgments

So many people, places and things became an integral part of the creation of this book. As I try to thank the long list of those deserving contributors, please forgive me if I do not name you specifically, but instead address you as a group. You all know who you are and how important you are to me. As I say to my kitchen staff, when I go to a table and the customer begins their praise of how wonderful MY food and the dining experience I gave them was, I very quickly correct them, saying that it is not all about ME. It never could be. It is about a team of dedicated people who have worked together with me and Delius to produce our vision as consistently and professionally as possible. My restaurant team at Ortanique Miami, Camana Bay and the team from The Dunmore hotel on Harbour Island have done just that. They helped me during my visits over these past few book-writing months in testing recipes, prepping items I needed, and lending their beautiful smiles to some of the lovely images throughout the book. I wish we could have used all those beautiful photos. The ones not used will be kept in the photo book of memories never forgotten by me and held forever close to my heart.

I also need to thank my wonderful students in my "Interactive Saturdays" cooking classes, who were the reason I created many of these "home cook" recipes with flair to begin with. You provided me with fun, laughter and a challenge to continually create new dishes that were fresh and doable. I am pretty sure we provided you with some of that same fun and laughter as well.

Now here is where some actual names come in. Thank you to my father, "Jolly Jack" McElgunn. He is no longer with us, but truly was a major part of my book. He taught me how to enjoy life and be happy. I tried so many interesting and weird foods with him that no one else in the family would eat. Brother John and sister Kathy were always the smart ones and got in much less trouble than I did, so eating strange things was a good way to kiss up to Dad. My biggest regret is that I didn't start this book in time for him to be proud of it.

Mom, you always were and still are the most amazing woman I know. I don't know how you put up with all you did, including me. We all enjoyed teasing your culinary prowess, or lack thereof, but you were right: we did not get skinny over it, especially me. You may not have taught me to cook, but you taught me to be a social butterfly and enjoy people and conversation with just about anyone. It is probably where I learned my people skills, and like you, I could talk the ears off an elephant. You brought love, life and happiness to our home and our table.

Everyone loved our house and you. Thank you.

Ma and Pa are no longer here, but not far away; always deep in the fondest of my memories, and I am sure the source of many of my life's lessons.

Justin, my eldest son, you were always my first little fishing partner. You love fishing; it is your pastime, your pleasure, your world and, hopefully one day, your inner peace. You will always be close to my side and always by my heart.

Christian, my middle son, you gave me one of the best gifts I have ever gotten to date: my Ortanique vegetable garden with the white picket fence you planted outside my bedroom window for Mother's Day. Who knew that tough-exterior son of mine had such a thoughtful way to say I love you. Who knew that was a sign of the farmer, hunter and fisherman you are today. I never know what you will text me a picture of next.

Last of my children but definitely not least, my pearl of a girl, Ashley. She has put up with her brothers for years and in doing so she has become so wise. She has stood beside Delius and me in this restaurant business for several years now, learning how to work in kitchens, giving of herself to charities, and showing up for the long, hard hours it takes to be successful. She has worked beside Delius and Ernesto, our manager, learning what it takes to be fair and contemporary, and to keep the heritage of a restaurant's reputation in the limelight through touching tables, social media and just being Ashley. Ashley, I thank you so much for the exhausting hours of dealing with my ineptness with computers. I am sure the techie world has it out for me; it is a conspiracy that my daughter has had to rescue me from so many days and nights during this book-writing process. I love you and look up to you; you work hard for what you want and believe in. You deserve the best.

Thank you Gil and Tricia Besing, owners of The Dunmore, Harbour Island, for bringing Delius and me on board as part of the Dunmore family. It has been a pleasure being there. You let us bring our crew over for six days for a photo shoot on the beautiful pink sands of Harbour Island and graciously allowed them to stay at your Harbour View Cottage. Such amazing accommodations could not have been duplicated. The use of your personal home, fishing boat and Captain Jermain for some additional shots provided a backdrop beyond compare.

Thank you as well to Tim Breyfogle for providing the perfect spot for our caja china pig roast in celebration of completing a successful photo shoot. It was the icing on the cake after a long day. You were a real sport to be the photography-crew boat captain on our fishing trip as well. It seems you don't just build shit, you also provide a great party house that comes along with an instigating brother, toting tequila shots, who somehow managed to get the entire party wasted before I even returned. And you are good with all that as long as we all get out at your bedtime. LOL.

So this leaves me with one hell of a huge thanks to give to everyone who was the driving force and flame under my ass to meet my book deadlines, who had lied to me about what the real deadlines were, and had patience with my lack of computer skills. Or gave me the occasional pat on the shoulder for confidence via email. That means you, Bob Morris, Ashley Fraxedas and Albert Chiang. Thank you so much Jen Karetnick; we finally did this. You have taught me how to write recipes so much more carefully, thinking of every detail I could be missing. You are wonderful to work with. And please, Ashley H., Delius and you are not to laugh, but I am so much better at the computer now. That I am actually proud of myself is another accomplishment, or wall I have climbed, with a little help from my friends and family. Thank you too Michael Pisarri for the gorgeous artistic images that so well depicted me and my personality, and Joy Moore for styling me and my food; you are so sweet to work with. I had a blast with you and feel that we will have a special relationship. Michael and Joy, Harbour Island will never be the same, you chicken chasers.

And my friend, my love, Delius Shirley, well, the dedication to this book was all yours … need I say more?

Index

Italicized page numbers indicate photos.